# BUSINESS INTERACTION
## E-mail

| | |
|---|---|
| **지은이** | 윤주영 |
| **펴낸이** | 윤주영 |
| **펴낸곳** | HiEnglish |
| **펴낸날** | 2017년 11월 30일 초판 1쇄 발행 |
| **참여자** | 서정민, Bruce Alexander |
| **디자인** | 정희정 |

| | |
|---|---|
| **전화** | (02) 335 1002 |
| **팩스** | (02) 6499 0219 |
| **주소** | 서울 마포구 홍익로5안길 8 |
| **홈페이지** | www.hienglish.com |
| **이메일** | broadcast1@hienglish.com |
| **등록번호** | 제2005-000040호 |
| **ISBN** | 979-11-85342-33-7 |
| **Copyright** | ⓒ 2017 HiEnglish |
| **정가** | 17,000원 |

All rights reserved. No part of this publication may be reproduced, stored in a retrieval system, or transmitted in any form or by any means, electronic, mechanical, photocopying, recording, or otherwise, without the prior permission of the publisher.

# Preface

**Business Interacion** 시리즈는 국내 대기업 및 대학에서 비즈니스 영어 교육용 교재로 많은 사랑을 받았던 비즈니스잉글리시 케첩 시리즈의 개정판입니다.

이 책은 글로벌 시대에 딱 맞는 커뮤니케이션 능력을 향상시킬 수 있도록 제작되었습니다. 다양한 비즈니스 환경에서 외국 오너들과 자신 있게 협력하고 의사소통할 수 있도록 실무에 자주 사용하는 표현과 어휘를 중심으로 구성하였으며 읽고, 듣고, 쓰고 말하는 능력을 키울 수 있는 기회를 제공합니다. 또한 비즈니스 환경에서 반드시 알아야 할 표현(expressions)과 어휘(vocabulary)를 소개하고 있으며 회화, roleplay, 연습 문제 등을 통해 내용을 확실히 익힐 수 있도록 합니다.

**Business Interacion**은 Presentation, Meeting, Email 총 3권으로 구성되어 있습니다. Presentation에서는 영어로 프레젠테이션을 매끄럽게 발표하는데 도움을 받을 수 있습니다. Meeting에서는 외국 파트너들과 효과적인 회의를 진행하기 위해 필요한 표현과 어휘를, Email에서는 직장에서 자주 쓰는 이메일, 회의록, 계약서 작성하는 방법에 대해 배울 수 있습니다. 그리고 QR 코드를 찍어 영상을 보면서 재미있고, 다양하게 학습할 수 있도록 구성했습니다. 본 시리즈는 무엇보다도 외국인들이 실제로 쓰는 생생한 표현들을 많이 포함하고 있습니다. 표현과 어휘를 중심으로 연습하면 오늘날 필요로 하는 글로벌 인재로 성장하는데 많은 도움이 될 것이라 확신합니다.

2017년 11월
윤주영

# Contents

| | | |
|---|---|---|
| **Unit 01** | **Promotional Emails** | 7 |
| **Unit 02** | **Requesting Samples** | 15 |
| **Unit 03** | **Sending Samples** | 23 |
| **Unit 04** | **Requesting Price Quotes** | 31 |
| **Unit 05** | **Sending a Price Quote** | 39 |
| **Unit 06** | **Filing a Complaint** | 47 |
| **Unit 07** | **Sending an Apology** | 55 |
| **Unit 08** | **Rejecting a Proposal** | 63 |
| **Unit 09** | **General Notice** | 71 |
| **Unit 10** | **Notifying Suspension of Service** | 79 |
| **Unit 11** | **Submitting a Report** | 87 |

| Unit 12 | Scheduling a Meeting | 95 |
| --- | --- | --- |
| Unit 13 | Cancelling a Meeting | 103 |
| Unit 14 | Meeting Minutes | 111 |
| Unit 15 | Follow-up Email | 119 |
| Unit 16 | Executive Summary | 127 |
| Unit 17 | Notifying Contract Termination | 135 |
| Unit 18 | Memorandum of Understanding | 143 |
| Unit 19 | Sales Contract | 151 |
| Unit 20 | Thank You Email | 159 |
| Answer Key | | 167 |

Unit 01

# Promotional Emails

## 01 Warm-up

1. Have you ever promoted your company's products? What kinds of things do you need to explain when you introduce your company and the products you would like to sell?

2. How much does the title affect your decision to open an email? Share good or bad examples of email titles and explain why you think they are good or bad.

## 02 Writing Tips

1. The "From" line should include both your company and name. Email from named individuals are more likely to be read than emails from "Info@ …".

2. Make the "Subject" line appealing by asking a question, stating a benefit, or sparking curiosity.

3. The opening paragraph is critically important to keeping the reader's attention. Offer the biggest promise or benefit to the reader upfront.

4. Include your contact details such as your phone number, email address, and postal address.

5. Avoid attachments. Many email systems restrict the size of emails, and many people fear viruses.

## 03 Vocabulary

### A  Word Definition
Underline the word with the given definition.

**1** using the most modern or advanced techniques or methods

You can tour our **state-of-the-art** facility and try out one of our fitness classes.

**2** to show or introduce a new plan, product, etc. to the public for the first time

The company hopes to **unveil** its new car engine at the annual Automotive Parts Show.

**3** able to be changed in order to be suitable for a particular object or situation

CL Electronics manufactures **customizable** hardware for smartphones where consumers can choose the capabilities they want.

**4** within a company or an organization

We are now conducting an **in-house** investigation into how the accident happened.

### B  Word Use
Write your own sentence using the underlined word in the sentence.

**1** Fresh Cosmetics launched a new campaign to **promote** its new line of natural cosmetics.

_____

**2** A consultant has been hired to assess how **cost-efficient** our manufacturing process is.

_____

**3** Our business has been in **operation** for over three decades.

_____

**4** The company has acquired a robotics engineering firm to develop their robotics **expertise**.

_____

## 04 Expression

**A  Opening a promotional email**
1  **We are pleased to inform you about** our high-quality car radiators.
2  **This is to inform you that** we manufacture industrial rubber hoses.
3  **We would like to let you know about** the recently released products.
4  **I'm writing to let you know that** we have recently opened a new online store.

**B  Introducing your company**
1  **Our company was founded in** 1962.
2  **Our company has been operating** in Seattle since 1967.
3  **We are especially focused on** meeting the needs of electronics companies.

**C  Introducing your products**
1  **We offer** a range of lending products to suit your business needs.
2  **Our company provides** industrial customers with cost-efficient electric radiators.
3  **Our company strives to provide** customers with quality air conditioning devices.

## 05 Mini Quiz

Fill in the blanks with the given words.

- We are especially focused on
- We are pleased to inform you about
- Our company was founded in
- Our company strives to provide

1  _____ a new festival concept.

2  _____ in 1992 as a spin-off company.

3  _____ the best service and product supply.

4  _____ providing personal services that respond to customer needs immediately.

## 06 Email Writing (1)

Complete the email by writing the given words in each blank.

- state-of-the-art
- operating
- rapidly deployed
- strives
- requirements
- in-house

Subject: The World's Best Radiator

To whom it may concern,

We are pleased to inform you about the high-quality car radiators made by High-up Radiator Co. We build car radiators (1) _____, and also take on outsourcing projects.

High-up Radiator Co. has been (2) _____ in Seattle since 1967. We are a member of the Mobile Air Conditioning Society (MACS). High-up Radiator Co. (3) _____ to provide customers with quality personal cooling systems and air conditioning services. We engineer our radiators according to your (4) _____, built to the highest standards.

We leverage (5) _____ technology and industry-leading expertise to provide utility and industrial customers with fully customizable, scalable, fuel-and-cost-efficient electric radiators that are being (6) _____ worldwide. Again, High-up Radiator Co. offers the most modern and trusted car radiators in the industry.

If you see something you like or you would just like further information, please contact us by dialing +82 (2) 555 6953 or email us at sales@highup.com.

Best regards,
William B. Smith
Sales Division Manager
High-up Radiator Co.
sales@highup.com

# 07 Email Writing (2)

Fill in the blanks with your own information and complete the email below.

Subject: _____
          your company's product

Dear Sir or Madam,

We are pleased to inform you about _____
                                    your product and its general features

made by _____. _____.
         your company        description of what your company does

Our company strives to provide customers with _____.
                                               your company's services

_____ We provide industrial
   description about how your company works

customers with _____ that are being rapidly
                the products that your company sells

deployed to everywhere in the world. Again, our company offers the most modern and

trusted _____ in the industry.
         the products that your company sells

Please have a look around our website at _____.
                                            your web address

If you see something you like or you would like further information,

please contact us by dialing _____ or email us at _____
                              your phone number                your email address


Best regards,

_____
     your full name

_____
     your job title

_____
   your company name

_____
  your contact information

## 08 Mr. Q's Email

Read the following and put yourself in Mr. Q's position. Then write an email using the expressions you've learned.

Mr. Q works for MQBattery.com as a member of the sales division and needs to write a promotional email to sell his company's products to electronics companies abroad. His company began operations in 1992, and is supplied within Korea rather than from abroad, which always comes with cross-border shipping and the associated duties, taxes, and customs brokering. MQBattery.com offers a full range of replacement batteries and battery chargers intended for most consumer and industrial users. The business sells various types of batteries, starting from $25. Their most popular item is the GPhyne 3G (Li-Poly type, AL-INP320CS 3.7v 1400mAh), which costs $25.

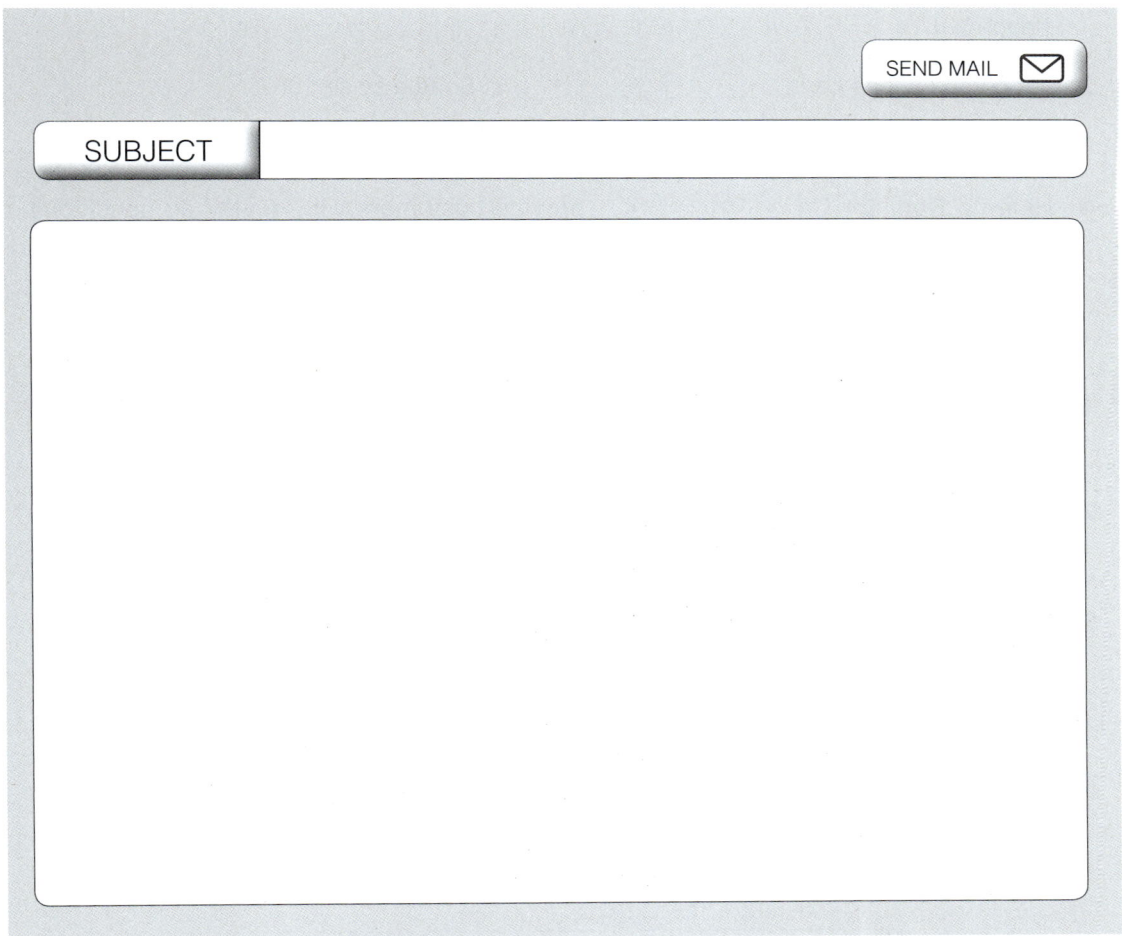

UNIT 01 Promotional Emails

# 09 Exercise

**A  Underline the best word to complete each sentence.**

1  A consultant has been hired to assess how (cost-efficient / cost-friendly) our manufacturing process is.

2  The company hopes to (conceal / unveil) its new car engine at the annual Automotive Parts Show.

**B  Fill in the blanks with the given words.**

- let you know about
- strives to
- state-of-the-art
- in-house
- operating
- suit

1  We are now conducting an _____ investigation into how the accident happened.

2  Our company has been _____ in Seattle since 1967.

3  We offer a range of rental products to _____ your business needs.

4  High-up Radiator Co. _____ provide customers with quality air conditioning devices.

**C  Put the words in the right order.**

1  according to | we | our radiators | your requirements | engineer

_____.

2  you | this is | manufacture | to inform | we | industrial rubber hoses | that

_____.

3  I'm | let | you | opened | a new online store | writing to | know | we | have | that | recently

_____.

4  you | one of | tour | and | try out | our state-of-the-art facility | can | our fitness classes

_____.

# Unit 02

## Requesting Samples

## 01 Warm-up

**1** What would you like to ask for when you request samples by e-mail?

**2** Can you think of anything else you need to know when requesting samples? Think about delivery schedules and make a list of the information you need.

## 02 Writing Tips

**1** Tell the reader exactly how many and what type of sample products you need and politely ask him/her to send them to you.

**2** Assure the reader you will pay any standard fees that are involved, if necessary.

**3** Provide a brief explanation as to why you need these sample products. For example, "We are currently seeking new suppliers."

**4** Be sure to provide your contact information such as your phone number, email address, and company website.

**5** Thank the reader.

## 03 Vocabulary

### A Word Definition
Underline the word with the given definition.

**1** a polite or formal demand for something

The city adamantly refused the request for payment since it was not legally justified.

**2** a company or person that provides a particular product

The U.K.'s leading battery supplier will open a service center next month.

**3** a product or service sold by a company, or a number of these considered as a group

The company broadened its offering of home health-care products.

**4** the state of being able to be used, bought, or found

The state-of-the-art data center ensures 99.9% availability all year round.

### B Word Use
Write your own sentence using the underlined word in the sentence.

**1** He's a very **well-known** and deeply valued businessman.

_____

**2** During the meeting, the consultant will **provide** feedback on the speakers' preferences.

_____

**3** The members of this **organization** commit to maintaining ethical standards in all business relationships.

_____

**4** An **additional** charge is made on baggage exceeding the weight allowance.

_____

## 04 Expression

### A  Requesting samples
1  **I am writing to inquire about** the product you advertised.
2  **I am contacting you to request** ten samples of your CCD image sensor.
3  **We would like to receive** a free sample of your CD335 camera lens.
4  **Could you provide us with** a sample of your product KS1001?

### B  Showing interest
1  **We have recently contacted** your company to draw up a contract.
2  **We are hoping to find a new supplier** as a distributor of our line of cosmetics.
3  **We are interested in establishing a partnership with you** in the image sensor field.
4  **We are also keen to** get a promotional brochure.

### C  Closing the email
1  **We eagerly anticipate** the opportunity to work with you in the near future.
2  **For further details, you can reach me at** jdk005@mqelectronics.com.
3  **Thank you in advance** for the sample.
4  **Do not hesitate to contact me** if you have any questions.

## 05 Mini Quiz

Fill in the blanks with the given words.

- We are hoping to find a new supplier
- I am contacting you to request
- Could you provide us
- Do not hesitate to contact me

1  _____ some samples of your products.

2  _____ for toy animals and other items in our shop.

3  _____ if you need further information.

4  _____ with an overview of your services?

## 06 Email Writing (1)

Complete the email by writing the given words in each blank.

- brochure
- manufacturing
- suppliers
- reach
- offerings
- request

Subject: XD-243 Motor Sample Request

Dear Mr. Daniel Lugo,

My name is Amanda Perry, and I am an engineer at Hi-up Electronics. I am contacting you to (1) _____ ten samples of your company's asynchronous motor.

My company provides electronic goods and is especially well-known for (2) _____ washing machines in Asia. Currently, we are seeking new (3) _____ of spare parts and components. We are very interested in finding out if your asynchronous motor, the XD-243, meets our needs.

Please provide details about the product, as well as any additional (4) _____ you feel may meet our needs. I would like to receive a (5) _____ from your company that shows pricing, availability, specs, etc. You can learn more about Hi-up Electronics at www.hi-upelectronics.com.

I look forward to hearing from you soon. You may (6) _____ me via this email address or by calling (056) 454-4564.

Best Regards,
Amanda Perry
Purchasing Department
Hi-up Electronics
amandaperry@hi-upelectronics.com

# 07 Email Writing (2)

Fill in the blanks with your own information and complete the email below.

Subject: Sample Request of _____.
                                              model no.

Dear _____,
        insert receiver's name

My name is _____, and I am _____ at _____.
                your name                            your job title              your company name

I am contacting you to request information on your company's _____
                                                                                           specific samples or services

_____. My company _____,
you are interested in                       description of what your company does related to your request

and we are seeking new suppliers. We are very interested in finding out if your

_____ meet our needs.
specific products or services

Please provide details about the products specified here, as well as any additional offerings

that you feel may meet our needs. I would like to receive a brochure that shows pricing,

availability, specs, etc. You can learn more about _____ at
                                                                                                 your company name

www._____.com.
           web address here

You may reach me via this email address. I look forward to hearing from you soon.

Regards,

_____
        your full name

_____
        your job title

_____
      your company name

## 08 Mr. Q's Email

Read the following and put yourself in Mr. Q's position. Then write an email using the expressions you've learned.

> Mr. Q works for MQ Electronics as an engineer and his company has plans to increase the number of megapixels in their cameras. Mr. Q must write an email to a camera component manufacturer called Cami Ltd. to request five samples of their new CS-300 digital camera lens. He'd also like to receive information about other camera components they might have and a promotional brochure.

UNIT 02 Requesting Samples

# 09 Exercise

**A  Underline the best word to complete each sentence.**

1  I am writing to (inquire / respond) about the product you advertised.

2  Do not (advance / hesitate) to contact me if you have any questions.

**B  Fill in the blanks with the given words.**

- well-known
- receive
- anticipate
- promotional
- contact
- provide

1  Please _____ details about the product, as well as any additional offerings you feel may meet our needs.

2  We would like to _____ a free sample of your camera lens.

3  My company provides electronic goods and is especially _____ for manufacturing washing machines in Asia.

4  We eagerly _____ the opportunity to work with you in the near future.

**C  Put the words in the right order.**

1  contacted | to draw up | have | we | recently | your company | a contract

_____.

2  a promotional brochure | to get | are | we | also | keen

_____.

3  am | to request | you | a sample | I | contacting | of your product

_____.

4  of our line of cosmetics | as a distributor | hoping | are | a new supplier | to find | we

_____.

22  BUSINESS INTERACTION  *E-mail*

# Unit 03

# Sending Samples

## 01 Warm-up

1. Have you ever received samples when you ordered some goods? What methods ways and what comments can you use to recommend other products when sending samples?

2. If you receive an e-mail requesting a sample, you might need to describe the samples in detail. What detailed information should you give to your customer?

## 02 Writing Tips

1. Thank the client for showing interest in your company's product.

2. Mention the price and list specific information on the samples such as the model name and number, color, size, material, etc.

3. Let the recipient know whether taxes and shipping charges are included in the price.

4. Provide contact information for purchasing or inquiries.

5. Close the letter respectfully and mention your appreciation.

## 03 Vocabulary

### A  Word Definition
Underline the word with the given definition.

1  to praise or commend (one) to another as being worthy or desirable; endorse
   However, I recommend that they are arranged in order to find information easily.

2  to make a new product available so that people can buy it or see it
   This release includes many enhancements and new features based on customer requests.

3  if something such as a bag, box, or place contains something, that thing is inside it
   The shipment contains all of the orders purchased by the customers yesterday.

4  the act or process of asking questions in order to get information
   I hope this information is helpful to the process of your inquiry.

### B  Word Use
Write your own sentence using the underlined word in the sentence.

1  All rooms have a flat-screen TV with an **integral** DVD-player.

   _____

2  American businesses rely on components to improve efficiency, reduce **lead time,** and trim costs.

   _____

3  We have created a new process to make clearer to our staff which of our pieces are **in stock** and which are not.

   _____

4  Price increases should be **acceptable** to, and affordable for, customers.

   _____

## 04 Expression

### A  Responding to a letter of interest

1  **I am writing in response to** your email showing your interest in our product lineup.
2  **We appreciate the opportunity to** send some of our samples for your review.
3  **Thank you very much for your interest** in our products.
4  **We are pleased to hear that** you are interested in our products.

### B  Sending sample information

1  **Regarding your request, I propose to send you** some sample inner tubes and our standard wheels as well.
2  Hopefully, these new powerful metal cases **meet your requirements.**
3  **The following is a guide to** important information in connection with our No. 2739 mortar.
4  **I regret to inform you that** our stock of the CS-300 lens is very limited.

### C  Conveying shipping schedule

1  **The lead time is about** two weeks from receipt of payment.
2  **Orders are shipped within** one week of the receipt of payment.
3  **Here is our shipping schedule** from our factory to your company.
4  The cargo **should arrive within ten days.**

## 05 Mini Quiz

Fill in the blanks with the given words.

> · Orders are shipped
> · The following is a guide to
> · The lead time is
> · Meet your requirements

1  _____ within 48 hours of being placed.

2  For mass order _____ about 15 days.

3  We can tailor our designs to _____.

4  _____ the navigation of your new smart TV menus.

## 06 Email Writing (1)

Complete the email by writing the given words in each blank.

| | | |
|---|---|---|
| • in stock | • inquiry | • receipt |
| • offer | • containing | • meet |

Dear Mr. James Scott,

Thank you for your interest in the KLW-335, KLW-336, and ECS-262.

These are crystal windows made from CaF2 with a filter spectrum.

The lead time is about two weeks from (1)_____ of payment as we have all of the requested parts (2)_____.

We can (3)_____ these at a special sample package price of 150 euros for each package plus three chips of each filter.

The total price of the shipment (4)_____ 9 detectors and 9 filter chips is 450 euros.

Hopefully these items will (5)_____ your requirements.

Thank you again for your (6)_____.

Warm regards,

Daniel Brown
Sales Engineer Sensor Division
Frontier Tech

## 07 Email Writing (2)

Fill in the blanks with your own information and complete the email below.

Subject: _____ Samples
           sample name

Dear _____,
       receiver's name

Thank you for your interest in our products.

As we have discussed before, we would like to offer you _____.
                                                          quantity of sample item

_____.
mention the unit price and list specific information such as model name and number, color, size, material, etc.

The total price of this whole shipment containing _____ is
                                                    the related items

_____. The lead time is about _____
the total price                              the period required for the item to

_____ from receipt of payment as we have all of the requested parts in stock.
be delivered

Thank you again for your inquiry.

Respectfully yours,

_____
your full name

_____
your job title

_____
your company name

## 08 Mr. Q's Email

Read the following and put yourself in Mr. Q's position. Then write an email using the expressions you've learned.

Mr. Q, the R&D manager at Cami Ltd., needs to write an email reply that they only have three samples of the CS-300 lens, which MQ Electronics requested. It will take more than six months to produce since the product was just released this year, so Mr. Q wants to ask if the delay is acceptable. Or, instead of the high-priced CS series, Mr. Q could introduce the cheaper MF-250 lens that is lower quality, but in stock.

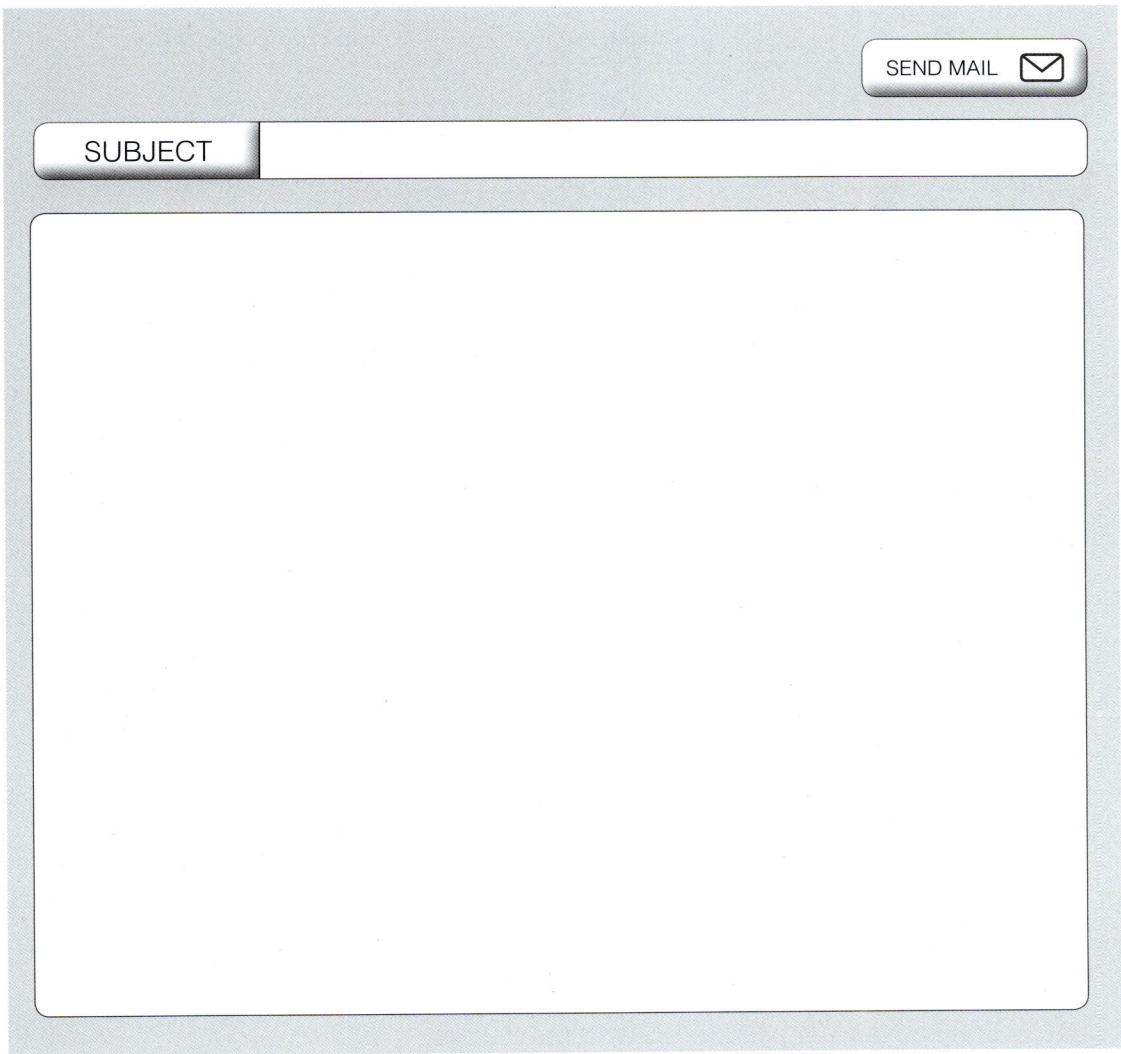

UNIT 03 Sending Samples

## 09 Exercise

**A  Underline the best word to complete each sentence.**

1  We are pleased to hear that you are (interested / ignorant) in our products.

2  I (regret / relief) to inform you that our stock of the CS-300 lens is very limited.

**B  Fill in the blanks with the given words.**

| • acceptable | • integral | • in response to |
| • release | • meet | • in connection with |

1  I am writing _____ your email showing your interest in our product lineup.

2  Hopefully, these new powerful metal cases _____ your requirements.

3  I would like to know if this delay would be _____ to you.

4  The following is a guide to important information _____ our product.

**C  Put the words in the right order.**

1  to send / appreciate / for your review / we / the opportunity / some of our samples

_____.

2  to your company / is / from our factory / here / our shipping schedule

_____.

3  propose / your request / to send you / regarding / I / some sample products

_____.

4  about two weeks / is / from receipt / the lead time / of payment

_____.

BUSINESS INTERACTION  *E-mail*

# Unit 04

## Requesting Price Quotes

## 01 Warm-up

1. What things would you consider when you write an e-mail to request a price quote? Do you think there is a best way to request a price quote?

2. Do you have any techniques or ideas that would affect the product price positively when you request a price quote?

## 02 Writing Tips

1. To receive correct and accurate quotes, make sure to clearly state the product name and/or model number in the request for quotation (RFQ).

2. Include detailed specifications such as quantity and your location to get better pricing and terms on the quotation.

3. Check for any additional fees such as taxes, delivery costs and packaging.

4. Establish a friendly relationship with the supplier's representative. It can help your later in both cooperation and communication.

5. It is a good idea to try to receive quotations from at least three different suppliers for future consideration.

## 03 Vocabulary

### A Word Definition
Underline the word with the given definition.

**1** *things that are produced in order to be sold*

Our company usually sends our **goods** to nearby enterprises.

**2** *a list of goods that have been supplied or work that has been done, showing how much you owe for them*

I'll try to get a list of the venders' **invoice** and get the rest from accounting.

**3** *a formal, usually written, request for something*

Investors must ensure that they include their e-mail address in their **application** form.

**4** *to show that a particular situation exists, or that something is likely to be true*

A recent study **indicates** that approximately 80% of employees are dissatisfied with their salary.

### B Word Use
Write your own sentence using the underlined word in the sentence.

**1** The VAT was also neglected in the final **price quote.**

_____

**2** If you have any inquiries or problems **regarding** your contract, please feel free to contact us.

_____

**3** Our award-winning system will alert you of any suspicious activity on your **credit account**.

_____

**4** I didn't feel that this was an **appropriate** time to mention the subject of money.

_____

## 04 Expression

### A  Opening a promotional email
1  **Please provide a price quote for** 75 office chairs.
2  **We would appreciate a quote on** the items listed below.
3  **Could you provide a firm quote for** these goods?
4  **Please quote your unit price for** the NSD-101 chips.

### B  Introducing your company
1  **Please provide us with your discount prices for** quantity purchases.
2  Please quote your unit price together **with your volume purchase price.**
3  Please provide a quote on purchasing RAM **in multiple units or large quantities.**
4  **Could you give us a reduced rate if we place a bulk order of** 500 boxes?

### C  Introducing your products
1  If these delivery costs are included in the price quote, **please indicate so.**
2  If delivery costs are not included in your quotes, **please state this clearly.**
3  **Please provide us with the following information regarding** any order that we might place with your company.

## 05 Mini Quiz

Fill in the blanks with the given words.

- I would appreciate a quote
- for quantity purchases
- the following information regarding
- We'd be glad to receive

1  _____ any relevant information.

2  _____ on the following items.

3  Please provide us with _____ our latest order.

4  To get our discounted offers _____ please email us the amount you need.

## 06 Email Writing (1)

Complete the email by writing the given words in each blank.

- price quote    • regarding    • prompt    • assistance    • appropriate    • result in

Subject: Price Quote Request
Dear Mr. Francis Garrioch,
This is Thomas Cruise, the purchasing team manager at Neat Furniture. My company is interested in purchasing the following goods:

| Product Code | NT 2417 | CQ 3233 | KF 6538 |
|---|---|---|---|
| Quantity | 1,000 | 5,000 | 2,000 |

Please provide us with a firm quote for the standard price for these goods, and state the time period this quote will be good for. Also, please provide us with your discount prices for volume purchases.

Additionally, please provide us with the following information (1)_____ any order that we might place with your company:

1. The standard terms for payment of sales invoices.
2. The availability of an open credit account with your firm. If available, please provide us with the (2)_____ credit application.
3. Any delivery costs for orders. If these costs are included in the (3)_____, please indicate so.
4. Any sales or other taxes. If these costs are included in the (3)_____ quote, please indicate so.
5. The usual delivery time for orders from the date of your receipt of a purchase order to our receipt of the goods.

We here at Neat Furniture have, in the past, placed orders with your company and have generally been satisfied with quality of your goods and in their (4)_____ delivery. As we have recently had some problems with our main supplier, a successful delivery of this order may well (5)_____ future orders from us for our supply requirements.

Thank you for your (6)_____ in this matter, and we look forward to hearing from you.

Sincerely,
Thomas Cruise
Purchase Team Manager
Neat Furniture

# 07 Email Writing (2)

Fill in the blanks with your own information and complete the email below.

---

Subject: Price Quote Request

Dear _____,
              receiver's name

I am _____.
            your name, job title, and your company

My company is interested in purchasing the following goods:

| Description | Quantity |
|---|---|
| model number or product name | quantity of the item |

Please provide us with a firm quote of your standard price for these goods, and state the time period this quote will be good for. Also, please provide us with your discount prices for volume purchases. Please provide us with the following information regarding any order that we might place with your company:

1. The standard terms for payment of invoices.
2. The availability of an open credit account with your firm. If available, please provide us with the appropriate credit application.
3. Any delivery costs for orders. If these costs are included in the price quote, please indicate.
4. Any clearance fees or taxes. If these costs are included in the price quote, please indicate.
5. The usual delivery time for orders from the date of your receipt of a purchase order to our receipt of the goods.

Best wishes,

_____
your full name

_____
your job title

_____
your company name

## 08 Mr. Q's Email

Read the following and put yourself in Mr. Q's position. Then write an email using the expressions you've learned.

> Mr. Q is the purchasing manager at MQ Office Supplies, and his company would like to start selling a new line of staplers made by Hi-line Fasteners. He learned of Hi-Line Fasteners' new line in their promotional catalogue. He needs to secure a price quotation for the standard black Hi-line stapler (model number HL1998), as well as for the deluxe red Hi-line stapler (model number HL1999). He'd especially like to know if Hi-Line Fasteners can offer free shipping for the order. He'd also like to know if staples can be included at a discount.

UNIT 04 Requesting Price Quotes

## 09 Exercise

**A Underline the best word to complete each sentence.**

1. Please provide us with your (increase / discount) prices for quantity purchases.
2. If these delivery costs are included in the price quote, please (indicate / refuse) so.

**B Fill in the blanks with the given words.**

- prompt
- standard price
- receipt
- stock
- quote
- supply requirement

1. I appreciate your _____ handling of these problems.
2. You should receive a written _____ for any repairs needed.
3. The _____ of the product has almost doubled due to high inflation.
4. The goods you recently ordered will be dispatched on _____ of the order form.

**C Put the words in the right order.**

1. could | for these goods | you | a firm quote | provide

   _____.

2. to receive | we'd be | any relevant information | glad | on taxes | shipping | etc

   _____.

3. appreciate | we | below | would | on the items | a quote | listed

   _____.

4. of 100 pieces | give us | a bulk order | you | a reduced rate | if we place | could

   _____.

# Unit 05

# Sending a Price Quote

## 01 Warm-up

1. Have you ever responded to a price quotation request? What extra things did you offer when you responded to a price quotation request? Share your experience.

2. What kind of expressions would you use to appeal to your business partners when you suggest a favorable offer?

## 02 Writing Tips

1. Open your email by greeting and thanking your customer for the opportunity to quote.

2. Ensure your letter has the company name, phone number and email address.

3. Include the following information for the quote: product name and number, quantity, shipping charges, unit price, total amount, possible discounts (if applicable), payment terms and shipment date.

4. If there are any price reductions for quantity orders, make sure to include them.

5. Set out a clear and logical structure and check your spelling and punctuation.

## 03 Vocabulary

### A  Word Definition
Underline the word with the given definition.

1  **to the advantage of someone or something**

Unable to borrow at favorable rates, the bank caused a series of global bank failures over the next few years.

2  **to tell someone that a possible arrangement, date, or situation is now definite or official**

I am writing to confirm a booking for a single room for the night of 6 June.

3  **a reduction in the usual price of something**

We're offering a 10% discount on all products this month.

4  **general and special arrangements, provisions, requirements, rules, specifications, and standards that form an integral part of an agreement or contract**

The average consumer does not read the terms and conditions that accompany the services they use.

### B  Word Use
Write your own sentence using the underlined word in the sentence.

1  I **placed an order** for a Hyundai i10 for delivery in June, following your advice.

_____

2  The center's **assistant manager** says she wants to address the factors that contribute to breakdowns.

_____

3  Citizens are wondering if they will ever be able to witness the **fulfillment** of the government's campaign pledges.

_____

4  Generally an adult passport is **valid** for ten years, such as one from the U.K..

_____

## 04 Expression

### A  Opening a promotional email
1  **This is to follow up on your request for** a price quote for the X100.
2  **I am writing in response to** your price quotation request for 500 brand sweaters.
3  **Please refer to** our terms and conditions below.
4  **We very much appreciate your interest in** our product line.

### B  Introducing your company
1  **We offer a 5% discount for** orders over 300 units.
2  **In view of the current trend of rising** yarn prices, we advise you place your order as soon as possible.
3  We are confident that you will not be able to **find a more favorable offer.**
4  **This offer is valid only until** July 5.

### C  Introducing your products
1  **If you need further information, please contact us at** 080-9911-8888.
2  **If you would like to speak with one of our representatives, please do not hesitate to contact us.**
3  **We advise you to confirm your order** as soon as possible.

## 05 Mini Quiz

Fill in the blanks with the given words.

> · request for a price quote
> · please refer to
> · see to your full satisfaction
> · a more favorable offer

1  _____ our terms and conditions below.

2  We are confident that you will not be able to find _____.

3  This is to follow up on your _____ for the X100.

4  We will do our best to _____.

## 06 Email Writing (1)

Complete the email by writing the given words in each blank.

- favorable
- securing
- exception
- place
- strive
- quantity

Subject: Price Quote for Wool Sweaters

Thank you for your email on January 3. We very much appreciate your interest in our products. I am writing in response to your price quotation request for 200 wool sweaters.

Please refer to our terms and conditions below:

| Item | Wool sweater |
|---|---|
| Product No. | PK 2339 |
| Quantity | 200 |
| Unit price | US$ 10.00 FOB |
| Total | US$ 2,000.00 |
| Shipment date | Within 28 days of payment |
| Payment | By irrevocable and transferable Letter of Credit |

We usually offer a 5% discount for orders over 300 units. However, as a way of (1)_____ future business and forging a lasting relationship, we are prepared to make an (2)_____ in this case and apply the discount even though your order falls short of our (3)_____ guidelines.

We are confident that you will not be able to find a more (4)_____ offer. However, in view of the current trend of rising yarn prices, we advise you to (5)_____ your order as soon as possible. While we (6)_____ to provide our products at the lowest possible prices, an increase in our production costs must unfortunately be passed onto our customers, a situation you can avoid by prompt ordering. We are looking forward to doing business and will do our best to see to your full satisfaction. If you have any questions or would simply like to speak with one of our representatives, please do not hesitate to contact us at 393-385-0404.

Warm regards,
Hubert George Baker
Assistant Sales Manager
Five Star Clothiers

## 07 Email Writing (2)

Fill in the blanks with your own information and complete the email below.

Subject: Price Quote on _____
                                  product name

Dear _____
      receiver's name

Thank you for your email on _____. We very much appreciate your
                             the date you received the request

interest in our products. I am writing in response to your price quotation request

_____.
               for the name and the quantity of items the receiver requested

Please refer to our terms and conditions below:

| Item | |
|---|---|
| Product No. | |
| Quantity | |
| Unit Price | |
| Total | |
| Shipment date | |
| Payment | |

_____. This quote is valid until
if your company can offer a discount, mention it here

_____.
       expiration date of offer

We are confident that you will not be able to find a more favorable offer. If you have any questions or would simply like to speak with one of our representatives, please do not hesitate to contact us at (555) 321-4949 or at sales@companyname.com

Cordially,

_____
     your full name

_____
     your job title

_____
   your company name

## 08 Mr. Q's Email

Read the following and put yourself in Mr. Q's position. Then write an email using the expressions you've learned.

> Mr. Q is the sales manager at MQ Foods. He was recently contacted on February 20 with a price quotation request by Alice Newman, purchasing manager for Desert Sun Supermarkets. She requested information about ordering 450 boxes of Raisin Snack Mix (product no. MQ1037).
> Mr. Q is writing back to inform her that the price for Raisin Snack Mix is $1.50 per box, and that MQ Foods offers a 7% discount for orders over 500 units. They accept payment by cash or Letter of Credit, and ship within five days of payment. Also, Mr. Q would like to advise Ms. Newman to order as soon as possible since MQ Foods' Raisin Snack Mix is extremely popular.

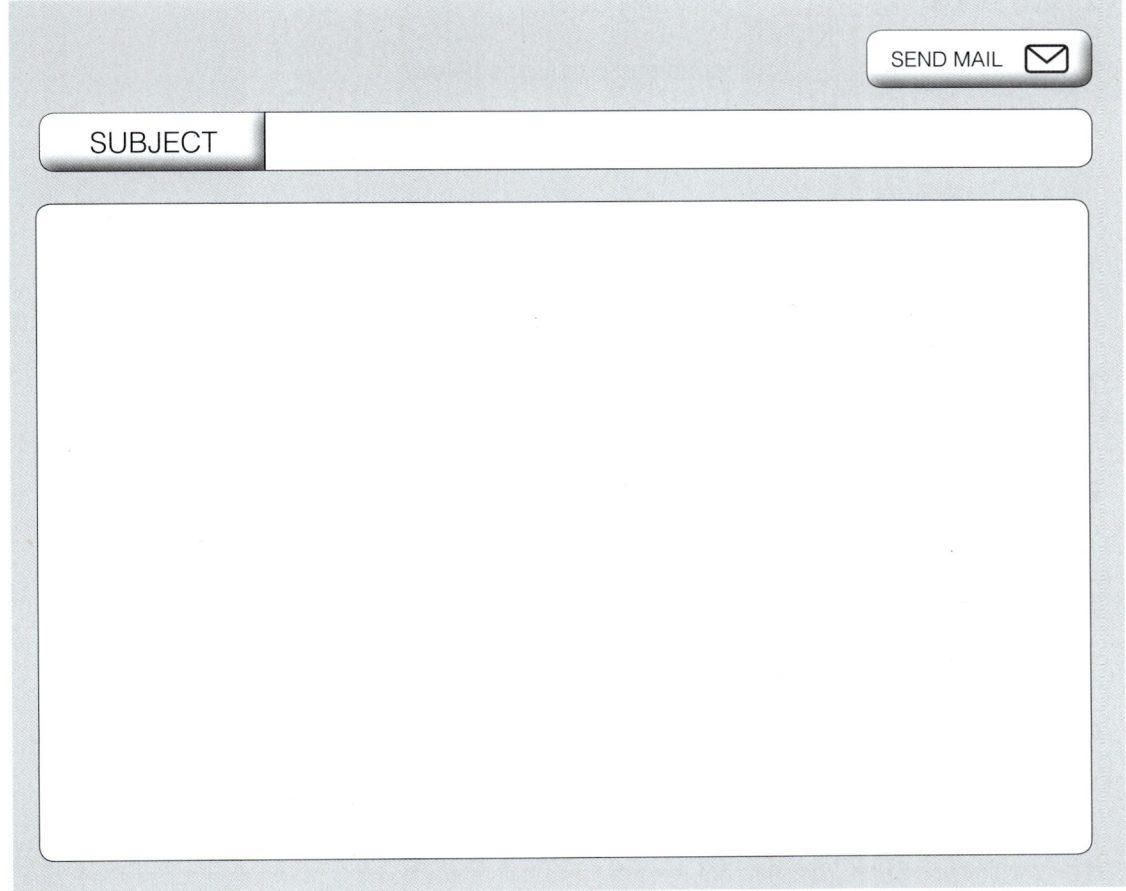

UNIT 05 Sending a Price Quote

## 09 Exercise

**A** Underline the best word to complete each sentence.

1 We offer a 10% (addition / discount) for orders over 100 units.

2 We will do our best to see to your full (satisfaction / discontent).

**B** Fill in the blanks with the given words.

- follow
- valid
- confirm
- interest
- refer to
- in response to

1 We advise you to _____ your order as soon as possible.

2 This offer is _____ only until October 15.

3 Please _____ our terms and conditions below.

4 I am writing _____ your price quotation request for our product.

**C** Put the words in the right order.

1 is | for a price quote | on your request | for our product | to follow up | this

_____.

2 at 080-1234-5678 | need | please | you | contact us | further information | if

_____.

3 to find | that | offer | not be able | we | confident | are | you will | a more favorable

_____.

4 to contact us | with one of | hesitate | would like | if | you | to speak | please do not | our representatives

_____.

46 BUSINESS INTERACTION *E-mail*

Unit 06

# Filing a Complaint

## 01 Warm-up

1. Have you ever complained with a written statement? How did you express your feelings, or what was your expectation when you filed the complaint?

2. If you have any experience handling a complaint or problem successfully, share your story with others.

## 02 Writing Tips

1. The tone of complaint letters should not be too aggressive, as this would insult the reader and discourage them from solving the problem.

2. Clearly state the problem and include enough details so that the receiver does not have to write back requesting for more.

3. Describe the impact this issue has had on you or your company.

4. Legal action is not normally threatened in the first letter of complaint, unless the situation is very serious.

5. Questions such as "Why can't you get this right?" should not be included.

## 03 Vocabulary

### A Word Definition
Underline the word with the given definition.

1 <u>problems caused by something which annoy or affect you</u>

   AIB apologizes to all customers for any **inconvenience** caused by this issue.

2 <u>fairly large, especially large enough to have an effect or be important</u>

   Your business should see a **considerable** boost in production throughout the holiday season.

3 <u>the difference between the amount you have and the amount you need or expect</u>

   Recently, European banks have been facing a massive **shortfall**.

4 <u>a quantity of goods that are sent somewhere, especially in order to be sold</u>

   Our company has received no such **consignment** note to date.

### B Word Use
Write your own sentence using the underlined word in the sentence.

1 We do not **anticipate** any problems with the delivery date we promised.

   _____

2 To our **dismay**, it turned out the sales representative lied to us about the price and condition.

   _____

3 The shareholders were **perplexed** by the sudden drop in stock prices.

   _____

4 If you buy merchandise online and discover a **defect** later, contact the retailer anyway.

   _____

## 04 Expression

### A  Opening a promotional email
1  **I'd like to file a formal complaint against** your customer service center.
2  **I'd like to let you know that** the goods we ordered **have not been supplied correctly.**
3  **I'm writing to inform you about a mix-up with an order.**
4  **I am writing to bring your attention to a serious issue with** your delivery process.

### B  Introducing your company
1  **The consignment arrived yesterday, but much to our surprise and dismay** it contained only 150 batteries.
2  **The goods we ordered arrived much later than we anticipated.**
3  **In checking that all the parts were enclosed, I discovered that two parts were missing.**
4  **This error put our company in a difficult position.**

### C  Introducing your products
1  **I look forward to your prompt response** in regards to this matter.
2  **I am afraid that we may have to look elsewhere in the future** for another source to provide our supply requirements.
3  **I would appreciate it if you could make up the shortfall immediately.**

## 05 Mini Quiz

Fill in the blanks with the given words.

> · make up the shortfall
> · file a formal complaint
> · much to our dismay
> · in a difficult position

1  This shortfall has put our company _____.

2  You should make plans now to _____.

3  _____ the consignment contained defective goods.

4  I am extremely frustrated with this situation and would like to _____ against your company.

## 06 Email Writing (1)

Complete the email by writing the given words in each blank.

- considerable
- correctly
- make up
- perception
- ensure
- fulfill

Subject: Re: Order No. 768197
Dear Ms. Mary Aughey,
I am writing to inform you that the goods we ordered from your company have not been supplied (1)_____.

On March 15, we placed an order with your firm for 12,500 ultra super batteries (code number AB1021). The consignment arrived yesterday, but much to our surprise and dismay it contained only 1,250 batteries.
This error put our firm in a difficult position, as we had to make some emergency purchases from an unfamiliar supplier at a higher price to (2)_____ our commitments to our customers. In addition to the greater cost, this caused us (3)_____ inconvenience in terms of both time and effort spent on part of our staff.
It goes without saying that this situation has not painted our company in the best light in regards to our customers' (4)_____ of our ability to meet their demand.

I am writing to ask you to please (5)_____ the shortfall immediately and to (6)_____ that such errors do not happen again. Otherwise, we may have to look elsewhere in the future for another source to provide our supply requirements, which is a situation we would rather avoid as we have valued our relationship with your company and generally been satisfied in doing business with you.
I look forward to your prompt response in regards to this matter.

Sincerely,
Allen Hunt
Purchasing Officer
HQ Goods

## 07 Email Writing (2)

Fill in the blanks with your own information and complete the email below.

Subject: About an Incorrectly Filled Order

Dear _____,
           receiver's name

I am writing to inform you that the goods we ordered from your company have not been supplied correctly.

On _____, we placed an order with your firm for
   the date you placed the order

_____. _____.
  the order's details       explain the resulting situation and problem

I am writing to ask you to _____ immediately and to ensure that
                   possible solution

such errors do not happen again. Otherwise, we may have to _____.
                                                         actions you will take

I look forward to your quick response.

Sincerely,

_____
    your full name

_____
    your job title

_____
   your company name

## 08 Mr. Q's Email

Read the following and put yourself in Mr. Q's position. Then write an email using the expressions you've learned.

Mr. Q is the purchasing officer for MQ Coolwear, a clothing retailer. He placed an order with HatTrend Inc. on February 2 for 600 baseball caps featuring the logos of three different popular teams, as well as 300 black and white earmuffs. The consignment code is number HN0161. However, when the order arrived, all 600 of the baseball caps featured the same team logo, and only 30 earmuffs were shipped. Mr. Q must write a complaint email to HatTrend Inc. to get the proper order within two weeks, before they run out of stock.

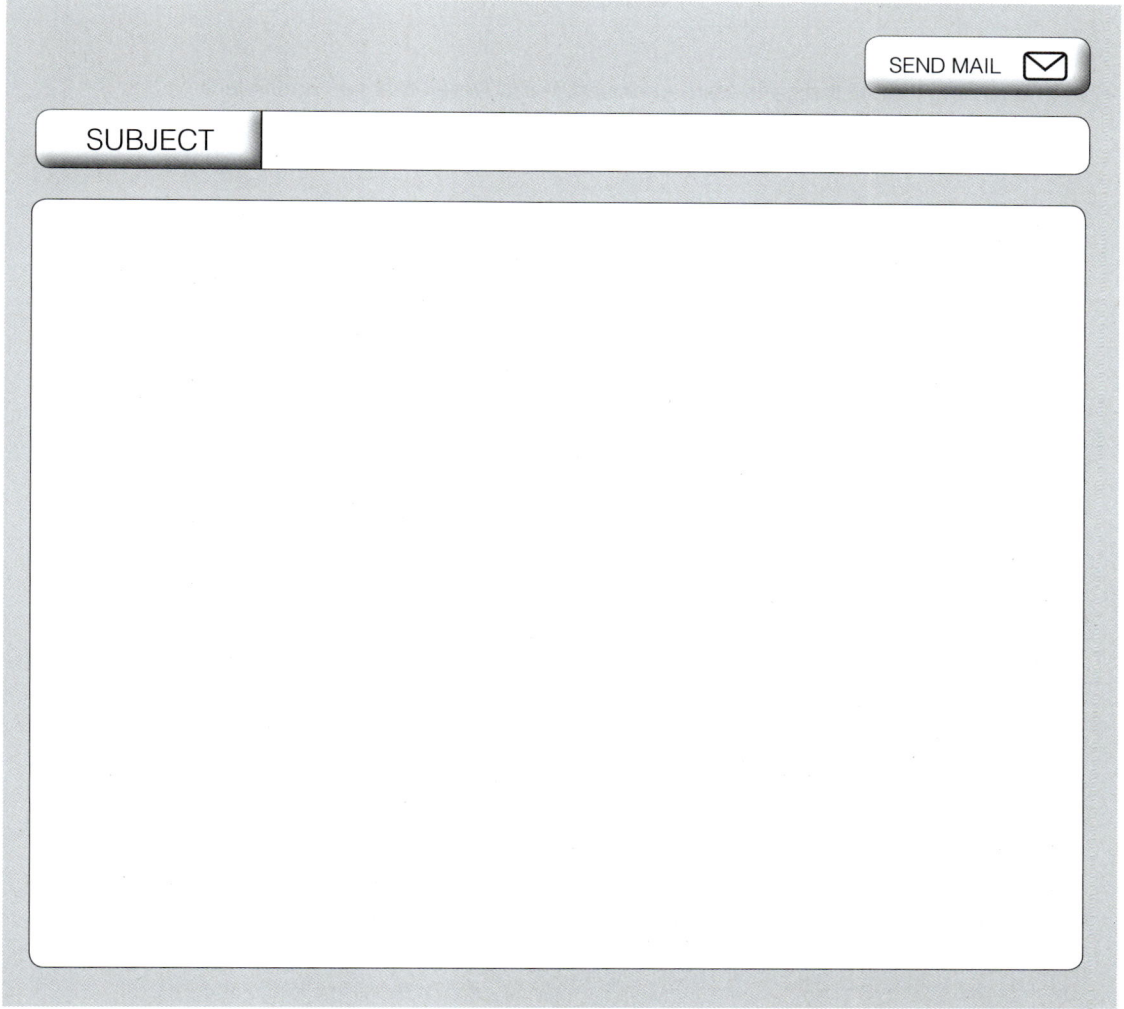

## 09 Exercise

**A  Underline the best word to complete each sentence.**

1  The goods we ordered arrived much later than we (precipitated / anticipated).

2  A (considerable / inconsistent) financial burden will be imposed if we don't close this deal.

**B  Fill in the blanks with the given words.**

- attention
- missing
- mix-up
- complaint
- consignment
- assurance

1  In checking that all the parts were enclosed, I discovered that two parts were _____.

2  I'd like to file a formal _____ against your customer service center.

3  We want _____ that such errors do not happen again.

4  I am writing to bring your _____ to a serious issue with your delivery process.

**C  Put the words in the right order.**

1  put  this  in  error  a difficult position  our company

_____.

2  the goods we ordered  let  know  you  I'd like to  that  have not been supplied  correctly

_____.

3  prompt response  this  look forward to  I  your  matter  in regards to

_____.

4  I  immediately  would  the shortfall  you  appreciate it  make  if  could

_____.

54  BUSINESS INTERACTION  *E-mail*

Unit **07**

# Sending an Apology

## 01 Warm-up

1. If you have experience handling complaints or problems, how did you apologize to your customers? How did you explain the situation to make the customers understand?

2. What kind of solutions or methods could be successful for addressing a customer's complaints? Would you provide any suggestions or alternatives if your company were at fault?

## 02 Writing Tips

1. Pretend you're the client and imagine what he or she went through. This will ensure the right tone is set in the letter.

2. Share the steps that will be taken to make sure the same mistake is not made in the future.

3. Offer the client some kind of compensation (either in cash or in kind) to make up for the error.

4. Close the letter respectfully and mention you would like to continue to work with them.

## 03 Vocabulary

### A  Word Definition
Underline the word with the given definition.

1  something that you say or write to show that you are sorry for doing something wrong

   The CEO issued an apology on the company's website to the customers affected by this issue.

2  in a detailed or exact way

   The lecture is regarding business, or more specifically small business.

3  not done deliberately

   It was merely an unintentional side effect of the meteoric growth.

4  the act of bringing back a law, tax, or system of government

   Citizens are fighting for the restoration of democratic rights.

### B  Word Use
Write your own sentence using the underlined word in the sentence.

1  The country's largest mobile phone operator **assures** service availability during the Christmas and New Year holidays.

   _____

2  The employer and employees maintain a close **association,** unlike other companies.

   _____

3  Security, flexibility, and reliability are among the top **concerns** for small and medium sized businesses.

   _____

4  We write this e-mail to offer our **sincere** apologies for the delayed delivery of your garment consignment.

   _____

## 04 Expression

### A  Opening a promotional email
1. I would like to **make an apology on behalf of my staff.**
2. I would like to **apologize for any inconvenience this may have caused.**
3. I'm writing this email **to offer our sincere apologies for** the delayed delivery of your garments.
4. It is with deep regret that I write this email to you.

### B  Introducing your company
1. I'm afraid that we couldn't fill your request.
2. We have been having difficulties with our delivery schedules lately.
3. Due to an abundance of orders recently, we had an unfortunate mix-up.
4. I assure you that **we are taking all the steps we can** to solve the problem.

### C  Introducing your products
1. We'll do our best to make it up to you.
2. Since our company values our association with our clients we are offering you a 20% discount on your next order.
3. I promise to ensure that it will not happen again.


## 05 Mini Quiz

Fill in the blanks with the given words.

> · offer sincere apologies for
> · on behalf of
> · with deep regret
> · taking all the steps we can

1. It is _____ that I write this email to you.

2. I assure you that we are _____ to solve the problem.

3. I would like to make an apology _____ my staff.

4. I would like to _____ the obvious disappointment and for any inconvenience that this may have caused.

## 06 Email Writing (1)

Complete the email by writing the given words in each blank.

- discount
- specifically
- association
- difficulties
- association
- steps

Subject: Our Apologies for the Delayed Delivery
Dear Mr. Henry Baker,
We write this email to offer our sincere apologies for the delayed delivery of your garment consignment (code number AL2135).

We are aware that you had (1)_____ requested delivery of this order by June 15, in time for your summer season opening day.

We have been having (2)_____ with our delivery schedules lately, and I assure you that we are taking all the (3)_____ we can to solve this problem.

Please understand our mistake was inadvertent. I would like to make an apology on behalf of my staff, and promise to ensure that it will not happen again.

Our company values its (4)_____ with our clients. Therefore, we are offering you a 20% (5)_____ on your next order.

In case you have any other questions or feedback about our services, feel free to contact me by email at amjones@pge.com, or by phone at +1 (404) 267-9982.
Again, Premier Garments and Exports would like to apologize for any inconvenience.

We look forward to continuing our valued (6)_____ with you.

Yours sincerely,
Andrew Jones
Sales Manager
Premier Garments and Exports

# 07 Email Writing (2)

Fill in the blanks with your own information and complete the email below.

Subject: Apologies for _____
                         the mistake your company made

Dear _____,
       receiver's name

We write this email to offer our sincere apologies for _____.
                                                          the mistake your company made

We are aware that you specifically requested _____.
                                              the item or service that the client requested

We have been having difficulties with _____.
                                       brief explanation on the cause of the problem

Please understand our mistake was inadvertent. I would like to make an apology on behalf of my staff, and ensure that such a mistake will not happen again.

Our company values its association with you.

_____.
 mention any additional benefits such as a discount that your company can provide to make up for the mistake

In case you have any other questions or feedback about our services, feel free to contact me by email at _____, or by phone at _____.
                  your email address                        your phone number

Again, _____ would like to apologize for any inconvenience.
        name of your company

We look forward to continuing our valued association with you.

Sincerely,

_____
 your full name

_____
 your job title

_____
 your company name

## 08 Mr. Q's Email

Read the following and put yourself in Mr. Q's position. Then write an email using the expressions you've learned.

Mr. Q is a sales manager at MQ Electronics. He must write an apology letter to Morgan Lawrence, the purchasing manager at ElectroMart. The most recent shipment of cell phones from MQ Electronics (code number MQ5513), which was supposed to be delivered on May 12, arrived at ElectroMart four days late. This forced ElectroMart to postpone a previously advertised sales event. The long delay was caused by a transportation error.

In order to maintain good relations with ElectroMart, Mr. Q is planning to offer a 30% discount on their next order.

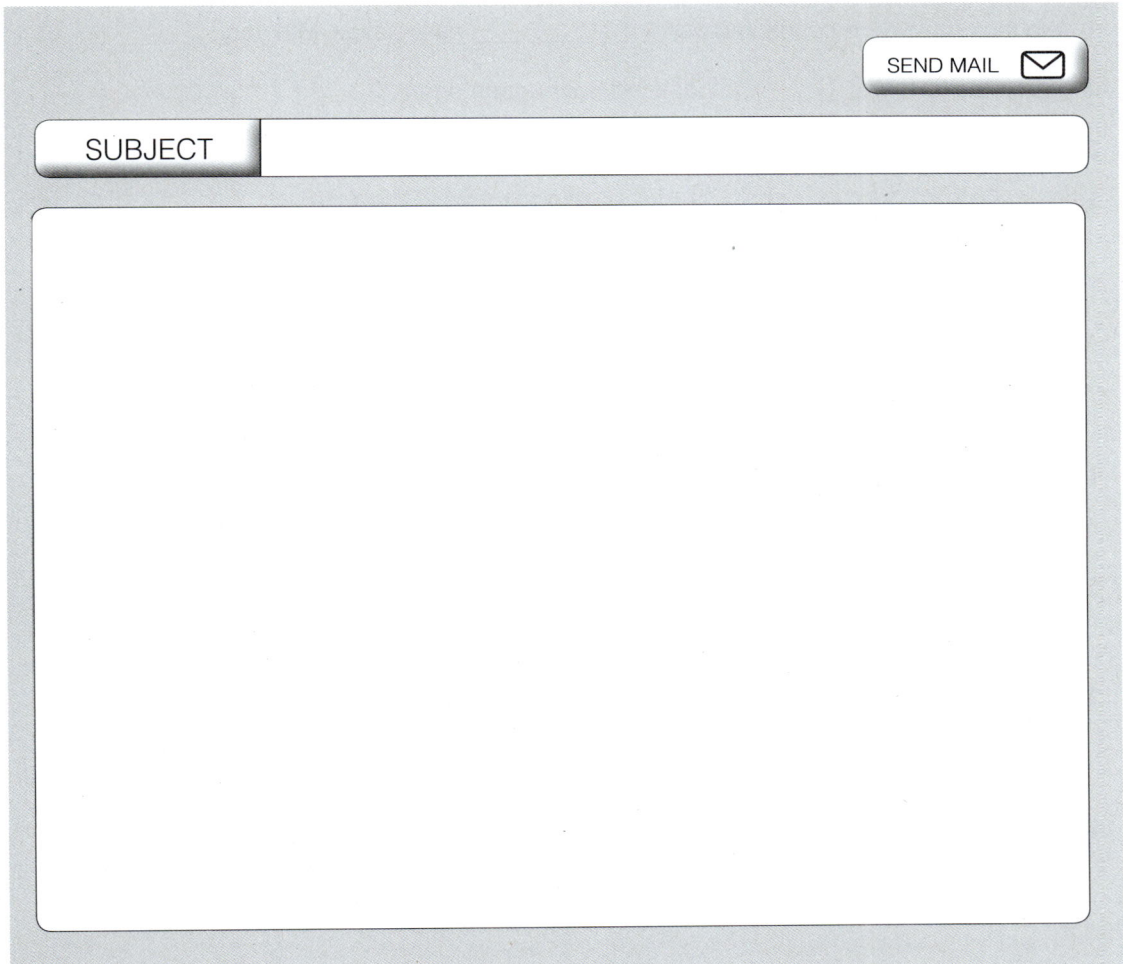

## 09 Exercise

**A  Underline the best word to complete each sentence.**

1  I'm afraid that we couldn't fill your (refusal / request).

2  Due to an abundance of orders recently, we had an (unfortunate / favorable) mix-up.

**B  Fill in the blanks with the given words.**

- behalf
- sincere
- valued
- regret
- apologize
- ensure

1  We look forward to continuing our _____ association with you.

2  I promise to _____ that it will not happen again.

3  It is with deep _____ that I write this email to you.

4  I would like to _____ for any inconvenience this may have caused.

**C  Put the words in the right order.**

1  on behalf   my staff   make   I   an apology   would like to   of

   _____.

2  lately   our delivery schedules   difficulties   been   we   have   having   with

   _____.

3  to make it up   our   do   best   to you   we'll

   _____.

4  to solve   I   taking all the steps   the problem   you   that   we are   assure   we can

   _____.

62  Business English Catchup  *E-mail*

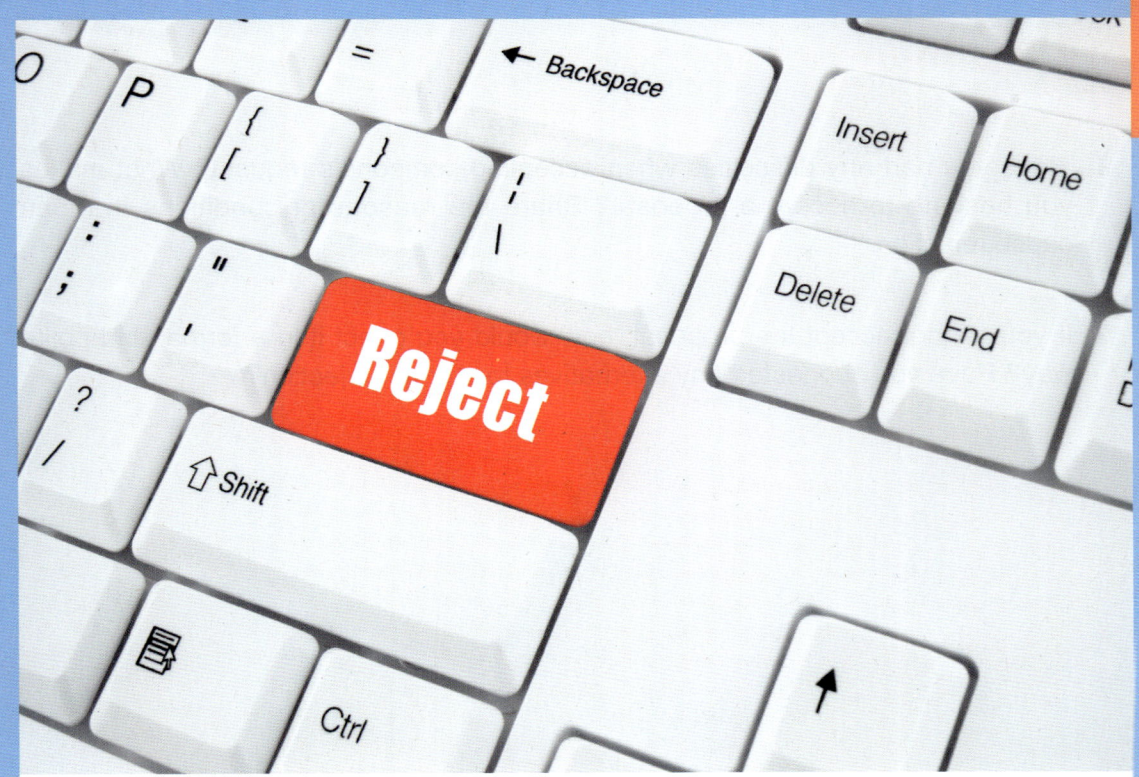

# Unit 08

## Rejecting a Proposal

## 01 Warm-up

1. Have you had any difficulties when accepting someone's request? What makes you hesitate to accept a proposal? Share the reasons or conditions that can cause rejection.

2. If you cannot accept the proposal, how would you reject it in a formal and polite way? Have you suggested any alternatives to outright rejection?

## 02 Writing Tips

1. Thank the recipient for the business proposal.

2. State the reason for the rejection. You need to carefully craft this statement as it can easily be misinterpreted.

3. Encourage the client to make further proposals in the future, or cordially sign off.

4. Thank the client for his or her interest in your company.

5. The manager or the company owner, if it's a small business, should sign the rejection letter and provide their title and contact information.

# 03 Vocabulary

## A  Word Definition

Underline the word with the given definition.

**1** a plan or suggestion which is made formally to an official person or group, or the act of making it

That business **proposal** merits careful consideration.

**2** of regulations, requirements, or conditions that are strict, precise, and exacting

We apply a **stringent** standard to maintain our excellence.

**3** a business deal or action, such as buying or selling something

The retail company stressed that they preferred cash **transactions** for small orders under 300 units.

**4** to work together with a person or group in order to achieve something

The upcoming meeting is to discuss how to **collaborate** with a web development team to promote our new service.

## B  Word Use

Write your own sentence using the underlined word in the sentence.

**1** I **regret** to inform you that the files you requested last week are not available.

_____

**2** He **assessed** the damage to the refrigerator that occurred while we were moving last week.

_____

**3** We updated our **pool** of suppliers since several on our list had gone bankrupt.

_____

**4** We have to analyze this data and complete a proposal within the time **constraint**.

_____

## 04 Expression

### A  Opening a promotional email

1  **I greatly appreciate your interest** in our products and welcome the opportunity to do business with you.
2  We **are grateful for your time and interest in** TR Inc.
3  **Thank you for your business proposal about** servicing and overhauling the machinery at TR Inc.
4  We **were pleased with your proposal** and **were impressed by** its terms.

### B  Introducing your company

1  We **carefully considered your proposal,** including the list of your most popular items and prices.
2  Our vendor management team has **reviewed your proposal** to ensure that it meets our requirements.
3  We **assessed the proposal to offer** your products and services in the next quarter.

### C  Introducing your products

1  **We regret to inform you that** we will be unable to move ahead.
2  Even though your proposal has enticing benefits, **it's not quite what we are looking for.**
3  We **already have a pool of vendors** who offer us similar services at cost-effective rates.

## 05 Mini Quiz

Fill in the blanks with the given words.

- grateful for your time and interest
- hope that we will be able to work together
- carefully considered your proposal
- regret to inform you that

1  I _____ again on other projects.

2  We have _____ and are not in a position to accept your offer at this time.

3  We _____ we have a prior commitment.

4  We are _____ in our company and products.

## 06 Email Writing (1)

Complete the email by writing the given words in each blank.

- investing
- reviewed
- move ahead
- appreciate
- accept
- constraint

Subject: About Your Proposal
Dear Mr. Joshua Harris,
Thank you for your business proposal about servicing and overhauling the machinery at TR Inc.'s new manufacturing facility.

As we have informed you, time is of the essence for this project and we (1)_____ your quick response in providing your proposal.

We are aware that the time (2)_____ our request placed upon you has led to some inconvenience for your staff.

Our vendor management team has (3)_____ your proposal carefully to ensure that it meets our requirements. However, we regret to inform you that we will be unable to (4)_____ due to our company's stringent vendor and cost policies.

Additionally, we already have a large pool of vendors who are able to offer us similar services at more cost-effective rates.

Although in this instance we cannot (5)_____ your proposal, we hope that we will be able to work together in the future.

We thank you once again for (6)_____ your time and energy, and for your interest in TR Inc.

Best regards,
John Moore
Director of Vendor Management
TR Inc.

## 07 Email Writing (2)

Fill in the blanks with your own information and complete the email below.

Subject: About Your Proposal

Dear _____,
            receiver's name

Thank you for your business proposal about _____.
                                                  receiver's offer to your company

Our _____ has reviewed your proposal carefully
      name of the team or person who reviewed the proposal

to ensure that it meets our requirements. However, we regret to inform you that we will be

unable to move ahead because of _____.
                                      the reason that you are rejecting it

_____.
  explain current situation or any specific reasons

We hope that we will be able to work together in the future. We thank you once again for

investing your time and interest in _____.
                                      your company

Sincerely,

_____
          your full name

_____
          your job title

_____
       your company name

## 08 Mr. Q's Email

Read the following and put yourself in Mr. Q's position. Then write an email using the expressions you've learned.

Mr. Q is the project manager at MQ Memory, a company that produces RAM chips for laptop computers. He recently received a business proposal from CompuSquare to collaborate on a new laptop model. However, MQ Memory already has a pre-existing contract with Nextcom Future that is still valid for two more years. Additionally, MQ Memory doesn't have enough resources to pursue another business agreement, so Mr. Q must decline CompuSquare's offer.

UNIT 08 Rejecting a Proposal

## 09 Exercise

**A  Underline the best word to complete each sentence.**

1  We are (doubtful / grateful) for your time and interest in TR Inc.

2  We were pleased with your proposal and were (impeccable / impressed) by its terms.

**B  Fill in the blanks with the given words.**

- collaborate
- analyzed
- transaction
- vendors
- benefits
- ensured

1  Thank you for your business proposal to _____ on a new laptop model.

2  We already have a large pool of _____ who are able to offer us similar services at more cost-effective rates.

3  We _____ the conditions and terms of your proposal.

4  Even though your proposal has enticing _____, it's not quite what we are looking for.

**C  Put the words in the right order.**

1  to ensure | our requirements | your proposal | that | our | has reviewed | vender management team | it meets

_____.

2  we will | regret | we | be unable | ahead | to inform you | that | to move

_____.

3  work together | hope | in the future | we will | that | we | be able to

_____.

4  your interest | I | and | with you | in our products | welcome the opportunity | greatly | appreciate | to do business

_____.

Unit 09

# General Notice

## 01 Warm-up

1. What occasions have made your work temporarily halt? What kind of information did you offer your clients of the standstill?

2. What actions should you take in order to maintain trust and prevent interference in your client relationships?

## 02 Writing Tips

1. Be courteous. You should address it to the appropriate individual so as to make sure the message reaches the intended recipient.

2. Keep your notice as precise and brief as possible so that there is no ambiguity.

3. Include the reasons for the notice.

4. Make sure that the action is conducted in a legal manner with as much reasonable advance notice as possible to the affected people.

5. Thank the recipient(s) and sign with the date.

## 03 Vocabulary

### A Word Definition
Underline the word with the given definition.

**1** a situation in which something is prevented from continuing in its usual way
Inevitably, prolonged hospitalization is a major disruption to a person's life.

**2** the support that you give a particular shop, restaurant, etc., by buying their goods or using their services
When was the last time a restaurant rewarded your patronage?

**3** when a factory, school, hospital, etc., has to close permanently
The report says that business' closure will create approximately 7000 job losses.

**4** directly relating to something that is being considered
There are probably many more things pertinent to your particular business.

### B Word Use
Write your own sentence using the underlined word in the sentence.

**1** The office will be closed **temporarily** due to redecoration.

_____

**2** Any software must be checked for viruses **prior to** its installation on computers in the office.

_____

**3** We are going to strive to finish this renovation in a **timely** manner.

_____

**4** Please note that our website will **resume** operation on the day following this Easter holiday.

_____

## 04 Expression

### A  Opening a promotional email

1  **This notice is a reminder that** we will temporarily close from August 7 to 11.
2  **We would like to let you know about** an upcoming interruption in our company services due to the summer holidays.
3  We'd like to **give you notice beforehand about** the unfortunate closure of our business.
4  Effective immediately, **and until further notice**, we will be outsourcing production to subcontractors.

### B  Introducing your company

1  If any orders need to be processed before then, we **urge you to place those orders no later than** July 31 to assure timely delivery.
2  We will **do everything in our power** to make sure that your orders go out on a timely basis.
3  We **recommend that you use** the cheaper X6-100 as an alternative.

### C  Introducing your products

1  We would like to **thank you for your loyalty and patronage.**
2  We **appreciate your understanding** on all of this.
3  **Counting you among our clients** is something for which we are especially grateful.

## 05 Mini Quiz

Fill in the blanks with the given words.

- is a reminder that
- until further notice
- no later than
- should you have any concerns

1  _____ feel free to call us at any time.

2  You have to send the manuscript _____ March 25.

3  The building is closed _____.

4  This notice _____ the following trials expired.

## 06 Email Writing (1)

Complete the email by writing the given words in each blank.

- following
- serving
- prior to
- timely
- should
- temporarily

Subject: [Important] Notice of Summer Holiday

To our valued clients,

We would like to let you know about an upcoming holiday at our company.

This notice is to inform you that we will (1)_____ close from August 7 to August 14.

We will resume business the (2)_____ weeks on Monday, August 15 at 9:00 am local time.

If any orders need to be processed during our holiday, we suggest placing those orders no later than August 1 to assure (3)_____ delivery.

We know this is a very busy time of year and we will do everything in our power to make sure that your orders go out on a timely basis.

(4)_____ you have any concerns, feel free to email or call us (5)_____ to the holiday for customer assistance.

We look forward to (6)_____ you again soon with our world-class products.

Kind regards,
Keith Oaten
International Sales Manager
Faith LTD.

## 07 Email Writing (2)

Fill in the blanks with your own information and complete the email below.

Subject: Notice of _____
　　　　　　　　　　　　summer holiday

To our valued clients _____ ,
　　　　　　　　　　　　or insert receiver's name

We would like to let you know about an upcoming interruption in our company services

due to _____ . This notice is to inform you that we will
　　　　　reason for interruption

temporarily close for _____ . The company will resume
　　　　　　　　　　　specific holiday name or reason

business _____ .
　　　　　the date your service resumes

If any orders need to be processed during this period, we suggest placing those orders no

later than _____ to assure timely delivery. We know this is
　　　　　last possible date to place an order

a very busy time of year and we will do everything in our power to make sure your orders go

out on a timely basis. Should you have any concerns, feel free to email or call us prior to the

holidays for customer assistance. We would like to thank you for your loyalty and patronage.

Kind regards,

_____
your full name

_____
your job title

_____
your company name

## 08 Mr. Q's Email

Read the following and put yourself in Mr. Q's position. Then write an email using the expressions you've learned.

> Mr. Q is the regional sales manager at MQ-Mart, a large supermarket chain in southern California. His San Diego branch will be closing for three weeks next month due to renovations. The store is to close on February 2 and reopen on February 23. Mr. Q needs to write a general notice about the temporary closure to ensure shoppers are aware of the closure and suppliers stop halt deliveries on January 31.

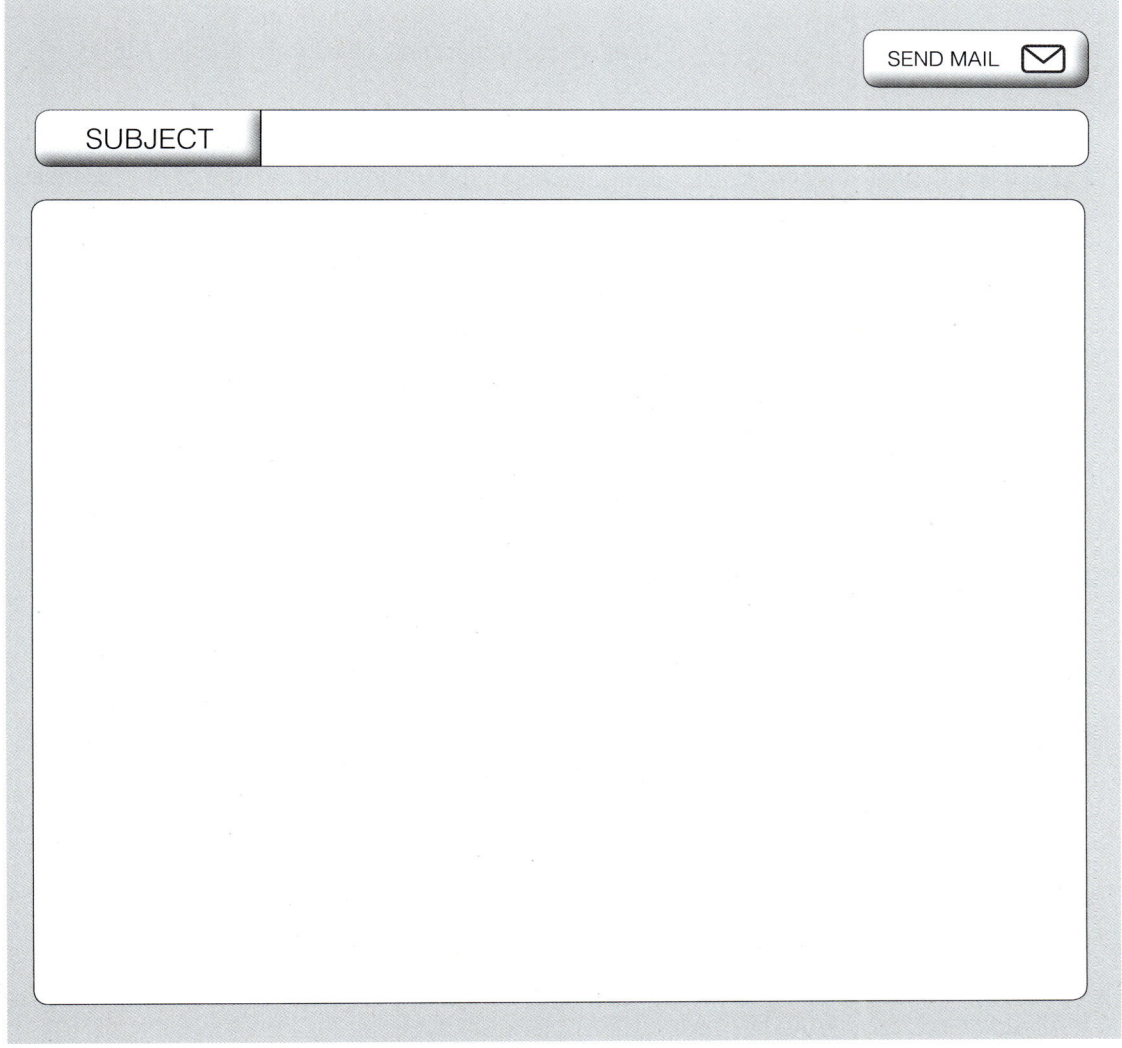

UNIT 09 General Notice

## 09 Exercise

**A  Underline the best word to complete each sentence.**

1  We (recommend / recall) that you use the cheaper X6-100 as an alternative.

2  Until (shorter / further) notice, we will be outsourcing production to subcontractors.


**B  Fill in the blanks with the given words.**

- appreciate
- beforehand
- urge
- interruption
- due to
- reminder

1  This notice is a _____ that we will temporarily close from August 7 to 11.

2  We _____ your understanding on all of this.

3  We'd like to give you notice _____ about the unfortunate closure of our business.

4  If any orders need to be processed before then, we _____ you to place them no later than July 31 to assure timely delivery.


**C  Put the words in the right order.**

1  your | and patronage | would like to | we | thank you | loyalty | for

_____.

2  we are | something | especially | counting you | is | among our clients | for which | grateful

_____.

3  in our power | on a timely basis | we | to make sure | your orders | will do everything | that | go out

_____.

4  you | the holiday | concerns | prior to | have any | should | to email or call us | feel free | for customer assistance

_____.

Unit **10**

# Notifying Suspension of Service

## 01 Warm-up

1 Have you ever received a notice about a service or production delay from your clients? If you have, did the notice clearly explain the suspension?

2 Why might companies have to suspend their production processes and what may allow their clients to continue their operations despite the suspension?

## 02 Writing Tips

1 Write which suspension is to be enforced.

2 Briefly state the reason for the suspension in one sentence.

3 Elaborate on the reason for the suspension in full in the next paragraph, if necessary.

4 Give notice as to when business operations will resume.

5 Include a warning against any repetition of the incident that led to the suspension in the future.

# 03 Vocabulary

## A  Word Definition
Underline the word with the given definition.

**1** to officially stop something from continuing, especially for a short time

The U.N. nuclear agency has urged Iran to suspend its uranium enrichment activities.

**2** something that you add to something else to improve it or make it complete

Nutritional supplements have become a billion-dollar industry.

**3** to make a process or action happen more quickly

I am writing to ask your company to expedite my order.

**4** a possible future effect or result of an action, event, or decision

The implication was that people would receive their needed nutrition from the pills.

## B  Word Use
Write your own sentence using the underlined word in the sentence.

**1** The CEO had **ongoing** meetings with his clients all week.

_____

**2** The new solar-powered factory will **facilitate** low-carbon growth.

_____

**3** Please note that our tour will **recommence** at 2 p.m., after the lunch break.

_____

**4** Possibly a very slight **adjustment** to their additional payment might resolve the problem.

_____

UNIT 10  Notifying Suspension of Service

## 04 Expression

### A  Opening a promotional email

1  **We regret to inform you that** our catering service won't be available **for the time being.**
2  The overhaul **will affect the availability of** some of our products for the immediate future.
3  **We apologize for the implications that** any temporary supply disruptions will cause to you and your customers.

### B  Introducing your company

1  **It is important to note that** the AccentU products you may have in stock from the facility are safe and effective.
2  The suspension of production at the plant **will allow us the time to** expedite maintenance and upgrade equipment.
3  The decision to temporarily suspend production **was driven by** the company's ongoing commitment to excellence.

### C  Introducing your products

1  Thank you for your understanding and **my sincerest apologies for any inconvenience** this adjustment may cause you.
2  We will **address the issues at hand and keep you informed of** any changes in the supply status.
3  While **it is not yet possible to** say exactly when product shipments will resume, **we will do our best to** recommence as soon as possible.

## 05 Mini Quiz

Fill in the blanks with the given words.

- are committed to doing all we can to
- will keep you informed of
- is important to note that
- will allow us the time to

1  We _____ developments as they happen.

2  We _____ bring this conflict to an end.

3  This _____ integrate this additional program into the schedule.

4  It _____ the expected impact might also be positive.

## 06 Email Writing (1)

Complete the email by writing the given words in each blank.

- suspension
- committed
- temporarily
- ongoing
- affect
- disruptions

Subject: Suspension of Service
Dear valued clients,

We are writing to inform you that AccentU International Ltd. has (1)_____ suspended production and product shipments at one of its manufacturing facilities.

This action will (2)_____ the availability of some of our products for the immediate future. It is important to note that the AccentU products you may have are safe and effective when used as directed on the package label.

The (3)_____ of production at the plant will allow AccentU to expedite maintenance and strengthen the site. The decision to temporarily suspend production was driven by our company's (4)_____ commitment to the highest quality standards.

We truly regret the implications that any temporary supply (5)_____ will cause for you and your customers.

While it is not yet possible to say exactly when product shipments will resume, we are (6)_____ to doing all we can to address the issues at hand and keeping you informed of any changes in the supply status.

Thank you for your understanding and support at the present time.

Sincerely,

Rachel Dobbs
General Manager
AccentU North America

## 07 Email Writing (2)

Fill in the blanks with your own information and complete the email below.

Subject: Suspension of Service

Dear valued clients,

We are writing to inform you that _____ has temporarily
                                        *your company name*

suspended _____ at _____ ,
            *the suspended facility*     *the facility's location*

an action that will affect the availability of some of our products for the immediate future.

The _____ produces _____ .
       *the suspended facility*              *the products that will be unavailable*

The suspension of production will allow _____ to
                                              *your company name*

_____ . The voluntary decision to temporarily suspend
   *reason for suspension*

production was driven by _____ . It is important to note
                              *further reason for suspension*

that the _____ products you may have in stock remain safe
              *your company name*

and effective when used as directed on the package label. We truly regret the implications that any temporary supply disruptions will cause to you and your customers. While it is not yet possible to say exactly when product shipments will resume, we are committed to doing all we can to address the issues at hand and keeping you informed of any changes in the supply status. Thank you for your understanding and support at the present time. Your company name truly values our business relationship with you.

Sincerely,

_____
*your full name*

_____
*your job title*

_____
*your company name*

## 08 Mr. Q's Email

Read the following and put yourself in Mr. Q's position. Then write an email using the expressions you've learned.

> Mr. Q is the General Manager for MQ Water, a leading producer of bottled mineral water in the U.S. They will be closing one of their bottling factories for two months from September 10 to November 10, 2018. The products that will be affected include their popular Fresh Sip mineral water, as well as the flavored Cherry Sip and Lemon Sip beverages. All of the waters from their Crystal Clear line will remain in production through another plant. The factory is temporarily closing in order to upgrade some equipment and enhance the facility to ensure it is operating at peak efficiency.

SEND MAIL

SUBJECT

UNIT 10  Notifying Suspension of Service

## 09 Exercise

**A  Underline the best word to complete each sentence.**

1  The overhaul will affect the availability of some of our products for the (immediate / implicative) future.

2  We will keep you (integrated / informed) of any changes in the supply status.

**B  Fill in the blanks with the given words.**

- adjustment
- commitment
- address
- temporarily
- recommence
- disruptions

1  The decision to temporarily suspend production was driven by the company's ongoing _____ to excellence.

2  We apologize for the implications that any temporary supply _____ will cause to you.

3  We will do our best to _____ as soon as possible.

4  My sincerest apologies for any inconvenience this _____ may cause you.

**C  Put the words in the right order.**

1  regret | that | our service | to inform you | for the time being | we | won't be available

_____.

2  doing | to resume | we | all we can | we can | as soon as | are committed to | shipments

_____.

3  facilitate | to you | will | the overhaul | surely | our services | in the future

_____.

4  us | to upgrade | of production | the time | will allow | the suspension | at the plant | equipment

_____.

# Unit 11

# Submitting a Report

## 01 Warm-up

1. How often do you submit or receive a business report at work? What is the purpose of the business report?

2. Have you ever been requested to write a business report? What was it about? How long did it take for you to write the business report?

## 02 Writing Tips

1. Explain that you are attaching the requested report as an attached file.

2. State when the recipient requested the report.

3. Briefly summarize the content of the report.

4. Be courteous and direct as the recipient is most likely a superior.

5. State that you welcome any questions the recipient may have about the report.

# 03 Vocabulary

## A Word Definition
Underline the word with the given definition.

**1** moving or reacting more slowly than normal

The economic growth rate was sluggish last year, showing the lowest increase since 2013.

**2** to become firm, steady, or unchanging, or to make something firm or steady

It is anticipated that inflation will stabilize at 4%.

**3** a question you ask in order to get information

All enquiries will always be welcomed about our services and polices.

**4** a group of people in a company or other organization who make the rules and important decisions

Mr Johnson, highly regarded for great leadership, was nominated to be head of the board.

## B Word Use
Write your own sentence using the underlined word in the sentence.

**1** One common strategy to create brand **awareness** is to make use of social media.

___

**2** Managers should set specific performance **objectives** for their teams.

___

**3** The book is **divided** into two very informative and easily readable sections.

___

**4** A company cannot be sold without the **approval** of the shareholders.

___

## 04 Expression

### A  Alluding to an attached report
1 **Attached is a copy of the report on** customer satisfaction.
2 **At your request** a copy of the report on last quarter's sales **is attached herewith.**
3 **Please find attached the report you requested on** September 9 regarding our factory's safety issues.
4 We submit the attached report on this year's clothing trend **for your review.**

### B  Explaining the content of the report
1 **The objective of this report is to** improve awareness of our stores and improve sluggish sales.
2 **The report deals with** the recent ad campaign for our men's skincare products.
3 **The report is divided into three parts:** Terms of Reference, Procedures, and Findings.
4 We've **referred to various sources** for the making of this report.

### C  Closing the email
1 **If you have any enquiries, please contact me at** sen@hiup.com.
2 If you have any questions regarding the report, **don't hesitate to contact me.**
3 We **welcome any and all feedback** from you regarding the report.

## 05 Mini Quiz

Fill in the blanks with the given words.

> · is attached herewith
> · attached is a copy of the report on
> · the objective of this report is to
> · once I have your approval

1 _____ of the final product I will send a request for payment to you.

2 A copy of the record of proceedings _____.

3 _____ provide a current overview of the market.

4 _____ the results of the investigation.

## 06 Email Writing (1)

Complete the email by writing the given words in each blank.

- divided
- upcoming
- awareness
- hesitate
- content
- attached

Subject: Report on Customer Satisfaction
Dear Mr. Johnstone,
This is Brad Chantel from the marketing department.

(1)_____ is a copy of the report on the market situation that you requested on April 21. The objective of this report is to improve (2)_____ of our stores and improve the sales of our laptop computers.

The report is (3)_____ into four parts: Terms of Reference, Market Situation, Problem Areas, and Final Recommendations. I hope the (4)_____ of the report proves to be helpful in stabilizing sales in the (5)_____ quarter.

If you have any questions regarding the report please don't (6)_____ to contact me at extension 4311.
We welcome any and all feedback from you regarding the report.

Best regards,
Brad Chantel,
Assistant Manager
MQ Electronics

## 07 Email Writing (2)

Fill in the blanks with your own information and complete the email below.

Subject: Report on _____
subject of report

Dear _____,
receiver's name

Please find attached the report you have requested on _____
date of the request

regarding _____.
subject of the attached report

The report deals with the _____. The report is divided into
summary of the content of the report

three parts: _____, _____, and _____.
first part　　　　　　second part　　　　　　third part.

We've referred to _____ the making of this report. We welcome any and
your sources

all feedback from you regarding the report.


Respectfully yours,

_____
your full name

_____
your job title

_____
your company name

## 08 Mr. Q's Email

Read the following and put yourself in Mr. Q's position. Then write an email using the expressions you've learned.

> Mr. Q is the production manager for MQ Motors. The general manager of his company, Maxwell Holmes, has requested a report from Mr. Q on factory safety standards. He wants to know how many industrial accidents occurred during the past year and how safe employees feel on the job. He also wants to hear any suggestions employees might have on how safety standards could be raised at the worksite. Mr. Holmes requested the report on December 10 and wants a report sent to him no later than December 15.

UNIT 11 Submitting a Report

## 09 Exercise

**A  Underline the best word to complete each sentence.**

1  The (representative / **objective**) of this report is to improve awareness of our stores and improve sluggish sales.

2  We've referred to various (**sources** / alternatives) for the making of this report.

**B  Fill in the blanks with the given words.**

- herewith
- attached
- enquiries
- feedback
- deals with
- divided

1  The report _____ the recent ad campaign for our products.

2  _____ is a copy of the report on customer satisfaction.

3  If you have any _____, please contact me via email.

4  We welcome any and all _____ from you regarding the report.

**C  Put the words in the right order.**

1  parts  divided  into  the report  three  is
   _____.

2  you requested  regarding  please  attached the report  find  yesterday  our sales figures
   _____.

3  regarding  you  to contact me  if  any questions  the report  have  don't hesitate
   _____.

4  herewith  on last quarter's sales  a copy  is attached  of the report
   _____.

## Unit 12

# Scheduling a Meeting

## 01 Warm-up

1. Have you re-scheduled a meeting due to unexpected or urgent problems at work? Share your story.

2. What information do you think is needed when you schedule a meeting with a written statement? Make a list and compare it with your partner.

## 02 Writing Tips

1. Request the meeting courteously and respectfully since you are asking the recipient to make time for you.

2. Provide any background information that you think would be useful to mention.

3. Be specific on why you want to meet and what you hope to accomplish through the meeting.

4. Give the recipient some specific options on dates and times and ask them to select one at their convenience.

5. Make sure that you mention your contact information so that the recipient can confirm the meeting when ready.

# 03 Vocabulary

## A  Word Definition
Underline the word with the given definition.

**1** not anticipated or predicted

The company closed due to unforeseen circumstances.

**2** to find a satisfactory way of dealing with a problem or difficulty

Chris was desperate for money to resolve his financial problems.

**3** the money that is available to an organization or person, or a plan of how it will be spent

Every division is implementing budget reductions.

**4** the process of changing something in order to improve it by correcting it or including new information or ideas

I'm making some revisions to the book for the new edition.

## B  Word Use
Write your own sentence using the underlined word in the sentence.

**1** Do you mind if I **drop by** this evening?

_____

**2** Today's meeting will **focus on** the new advertising campaign.

_____

**3** Customers who have an **appointment** with PG&E will receive a call back.

_____

**4** I sincerely hope that the resolutions made at this conference will **go a long way** toward enhancing the quality of education in our various institutions.

_____

## 04 Expression

### A  Requesting a meeting
1  Why don't we schedule a meeting **to discuss this further?**
2  If you have time, **could we schedule a meeting so as to** discuss this matter in more detail?
3  Why don't we **follow up the discussion we had with a meeting on** Thursday?
4  If it's OK with you, I'll **drop by your office on** Tuesday morning for a meeting.

### B  Stating objectives for the meeting
1  **The meeting will go a long way in** resolving our budget issues.
2  **This is to discuss** the ongoing project and what changes we can make to current plans.
3  **The meeting will focus on** the local building code, which was recently revised.
4  **The list of things I would like to cover includes** the following: safety issues, budget concerns, and sales contracts.

### C  Closing the email
1  Please **let me know when you are available** this week.
2  I'll contact you again next week **to schedule an appointment.**
3  I will call your office **to inquire about a convenient time and place for the meeting.**
4  Please **confirm the date and time** at your earliest convenience.


## 05 Mini Quiz

Fill in the blanks with the given words.

- to follow up the discussion
- to confirm the date and time
- the meeting will focus on
- to discuss this further

1  _____ trading and investment as means of promoting sustainable development.

2  I would like _____ on the matter at the meeting on 12 March.

3  Perhaps we should meet again _____.

4  Send them an email _____ of the meeting and set final details.

## 06 Email Writing (1)

Complete the email by writing the given words in each blank.

- resolving
- changed
- convenience
- unforeseen
- detail
- planned

Subject: Request for Meeting

Dear Ms. Emily Wainwright,

As you know, our construction project has been going ahead as (1)_____ but there have been some (2)_____ changes. Apparently the local building code regarding weight-bearing walls was recently (3)_____ and requires a revision in our construction plans.

If you have time next week, could we schedule a meeting so as to discuss this matter in more (4)_____?

The meeting will go a long way in (5)_____ prickly issues regarding the building code.

I am free on Monday and Wednesday morning, and any day except Tuesday in the evenings after 6 p.m.

Please confirm a date and time at your earliest (6)_____.

Yours truly,

Derrick Harmon
Account Director
Horizon Architects

## 07 Email Writing (2)

Fill in the blanks with your own information and complete the email below.

Subject: Scheduling a Meeting

Dear _____,
     name of recipient

This is to inform you that _____.
                          a matter needs to be discussed

_____. The cost to work around these problems is
give extra information about the problem, if possible

estimated at _____.
              estimated cost of solution

If you have time _____, could we schedule a meeting
                 time you want to schedule the meeting

so as to discuss this matter in detail? I am also free on _____.
                                                          days and times you are available

My phone number is _____, and my email address is
                   your phone number

_____. Please let me know when you are available.
your email address

Sincerely,

_____
your full name

_____
your job position

_____
your company name

## 08 Mr. Q's Email

Read the following and put yourself in Mr. Q's position. Then write an email using the expressions you've learned.

> Mr. Q is the accounting director at MQ Landscaping. The company has run into some difficulties while installing a swimming pool for a new resort. There are underground electric cables and sewage pipes that need to be rerouted before the pool can go in. The estimated cost to work around this problem is an extra $30,000.
>
> Mr. Q needs to contact Barbara Dickens, the account manager for Sun Resorts, to schedule a meeting to discuss this matter. Mr. Q is available in the mornings before 11 a.m. every weekday except Fridays, and on Mondays and Tuesdays after 6 p.m. His phone number is +8 (010) 5511-2266, and his email address is misterq@mq.com.

**SEND MAIL**

**SUBJECT**

UNIT 12 Scheduling a Meeting

## 09 Exercise

**A  Underline the best word to complete each sentence.**

1  Why don't we (reroute / follow) up the discussion we had with a meeting on Thursday?

2  Why don't we schedule a meeting to (discuss / dissolve) this further?

**B  Fill in the blanks with the given words.**

- cover
- set aside
- drop by
- resolving
- work around
- focus on

1  If it's OK with you, I'll _____ your office on Thursday for a meeting.

2  The meeting will go a long way in _____ our security issues.

3  The meeting will _____ the local building code which was recently revised.

4  The list of things I would like to _____ includes the following: safety issues, budget concerns, and sales contracts.

**C  Put the words in the right order.**

1  I'll | to schedule | you | contact | next week | again | an appointment

    _____.

2  the ongoing project | this is | to discuss | and | we can make | what changes | to current plans

    _____.

3  please | know | this week | let me | when | available | you are

    _____.

4  your office | I will | for the meeting | and place | to inquire about | call | a convenient | time

    _____.

Unit **13**

# Cancelling a Meeting

## 01 Warm-up

1. Have you ever cancelled a meeting before? What kind of reasons did you provide for making the cancellation and how specifically did you explain the situation to excuse your self?

2. When you reschedule a meeting, what should you notify the e-mail recipients of? How can you to prepare in advance for the event that the recipients do not come on the revised date?

## 02 Writing Tips

1. Apologize and tell them you understand the inconvenience it may cause them.

2. Explain the reason for postponing or cancelling the event in detail, without going into too many specifics.

3. Try to reschedule the meeting right away.

4. Make sure they understand that you are opening up your schedule to work around theirs.

5. Make up for your cancellation by making your next meeting as pleasant as possible for the other person, like preparing fresh water, coffee, or snacks.

# 03 Vocabulary

## A Word Definition
Underline the word with the given definition.

**1** a problem that delays or prevents progress, or makes things worse than they were

Don't worry too much about this delay because there is no business success without setbacks.

**2** the condition in which you live, especially how much money you have

Due to unforeseen circumstances, we decided not to acquire Florida Beach Hotel.

**3** impossible to prevent

Considering the low birth rate, it is unavoidable that Korea will become an aged society.

**4** to change the date or time of a planned event or action to a later one

Did they say why they want to postpone the demonstration?

## B Word Use
Write your own sentence using the underlined word in the sentence.

**1** Parents must **set aside** time to listen to their children.

_____

**2** Because of lack of funds, the project was **put on hold**.

_____

**3** Over a hundred people were in **attendance** at the meeting.

_____

**4** The subject of the talk is announced a week **in advance**.

_____

UNIT 13 Cancelling a Meeting

# 04 Expression

### A  Notifying of cancellation

1  **I apologize for the inconvenience but** we need to reschedule tomorrow's meeting.
2  **Due to unexpected circumstances,** the meeting originally scheduled for March 6 was cancelled.
3  Unfortunately an issue that came up **has forced us to** cancel the writing conference.
4  A sudden turn of events will **prevent us from going ahead with the meeting.**

### B  Rescheduling a meeting

1  I'm afraid the date of the meeting **has been moved to** January 21.
2  The meeting has been **postponed until** Friday.
3  Please **set aside** the new date of June 6, on your calendar.
4  The meeting **has been put on hold until further notice.**

### C  Closing the email

1  Please let us know of **your available dates for the meeting.**
2  Please **advise us of your availability for attendance.**
3  **Once again, we would like to apologize for the delay** and we hope to see you on May 2.
4  I thank you in advance **for your patience and understanding.**


# 05 Mini Quiz

Fill in the blanks with the given words.

- due to unexpected circumstances
- for your patience and understanding
- has been moved to
- has forced us to

1  I'd like to thank you all _____

2  _____, the seminar will start two weeks later than announced.

3  The change _____ look at these things again.

4  Please note that election day _____ May 9th.

106  **BUSINESS INTERACTION** *E-mail*

## 06 Email Writing (1)

Complete the email by writing the given words in each blank.

- unexpected
- following
- less
- originally
- until
- setback

Subject: Postponement of the AGM

Dear Mr. Edward Mahoney,

Due to (1)_____ circumstances, the AGM (2)_____ scheduled for March 16 was delayed.

This is due to an unexpected delay with the production of the annual report which was on schedule up until last week. This (3)_____, although unavoidable, is regretted.

However, it was felt that holding the AGM without the annual report would be (4)_____ than ideal. Therefore, the meeting has been postponed (5)_____ Friday, May 2.

The meeting is expected to last until late afternoon. Lunch will be provided, as well as a dinner (6)_____ the meeting.

Once again, we apologize for the delay and we hope to see you on May 2.

Sincerely,

Martin Pike
Managing Director
AccentU International LTD.

# 07 Email Writing (2)

Fill in the blanks with your own information and complete the email below.

Subject: Postponement of _____
                          of name of event

Dear _____ ,
       name of receiver

I regret to inform you that the _____ scheduled for
                                  name of event being postponed

_____ will be postponed due to _____
  date of event                               reason for delay

_____.
explain the reason for postponing the event in greater detail, without going into too many specifics

This setback, although unavoidable, is regretted. However, it was felt that holding the

_____ without the _____
  name of event                  what is missing or reason for delay

would be less than ideal.

The new date that has been set aside for the _____ is
                                                event name

_____ , and will take place at event location beginning at _____.
new date of event,                                                      starting time of event

The event is expected to last until _____. Once again, we would like to
                                      ending time of event

apologize for the delay and we hope to see you on _____.
                                                    new date of event

Cordially,

_____
your full name

_____
your job title

_____
your company name

108  BUSINESS INTERACTION  *E-mail*

## 08 Mr. Q's Email

Read the following and put yourself in Mr. Q's position. Then write an email using the expressions you've learned.

> Mr. Q is the managing director of MQ Games, a video game company. He must write a notice that the company's upcoming product launch event for their much-anticipated game, "Power Smash", will be delayed six months due to problems encountered during game development. MQ Games does not feel that Power Smash is ready for release, and that launching it later will result in a better game and a sales increase. The event was supposed to take place on May 19. The event will now take place on November 7, at the Next Plaza Exhibition Center in downtown San Francisco from 10 a.m. until 6 p.m.

**SEND MAIL**

**SUBJECT**

## 09 Exercise

**A  Underline the best word to complete each sentence.**

1  I (apologize / anticipate) for the inconvenience, but we need to reschedule tomorrow's meeting.

2  Unfortunately, an issue that came up has (forced / encouraged) us to cancel the conference.

**B  Fill in the blanks with the given words.**

- apologize
- patience
- set aside
- postpone
- available
- prevent

1  Please let us know of your _____ dates for the meeting.

2  A sudden turn of events will _____ us from going ahead with the meeting.

3  I thank you in advance for your _____ and understanding.

4  Please _____ the new date of June 6 on your calendar.

**C  Put the words in the right order.**

1  put on hold | has | until | the meeting | notice | been | further

_____.

2  of | us | please | advise | for attendance | your availability

_____.

3  we | apologize | once again | on May 2 | to see you | for the delay | would like to | and we hope

_____.

4  circumstances | unexpected | for March 6 | due to | was cancelled | originally | scheduled | the meeting

_____.

110  BUSINESS INTERACTION  *E-mail*

Unit **14**

# Meeting Minutes

## 01 Warm-up

1. The minutes of a meeting are meant to be an official version of what transpired during the meeting. Why do you think an organization needs to take the minutes of a meeting, and why should they be kept?

2. What pertinent information should be included when you take the minutes of a meeting? How do you record the minutes to provide a thorough and accurate account?

## 02 Writing Tips

1. Be concise and accurate.

2. Make sure to write down details such as the date and time of the meeting, names of the people who attended, and all the issues that were discussed.

3. Be objective and write in the same tense throughout. The fewer adjectives or adverbs you use, the better.

4. Include all the decisions that were made.

5. After writing the minutes, go over your notes again to make sure everything is accurate, and then send them to the relevant people.

## 03 Vocabulary

### A Word Definition
Underline the word with the given definition.

1 to be in charge of a formal event, organization, ceremony, etc.
The annual sales meeting was presided over by Ms. Alexander, our sales team manager.

2 come or bring together for a meeting or activity; assemble
The committee meeting was convened at 10 a.m. last Friday in the main conference hall.

3 a small change made in something such as a design, plan, or system
The following document should be completed without modification to the template.

4 an official written record of what is said and decided at a meeting
Amy Allison was asked to attend to the board meeting as the minutes taker.

### B Word Use
Write your own sentence using the underlined word in the sentence.

1 The executive management agreed to carry the **resolution** to downsize the current staff by 5%.

_____

2 The shareholder meeting is supposed to be **adjourned** before lunch.

_____

3 The **motion** to hold a welcoming reception for volunteers was carried unanimously.

_____

4 The conference **approved** a proposal for a referendum.

_____

## 04 Expression

### A  Writing the introduction
1. The management meeting **was presided over by** Abigail Niehaus.
2. Meeting **convened at** 9:30 a.m., Chairman Sidney Loups presiding.
3. The chairperson **called the meeting to order at** 10 a.m.
4. **Meeting called to order at** 12:00 p.m. **by** chair Taylor Cooper.

### B  Summarizing discussions
1. Minutes from the meeting on April 21 were **approved without modification.**
2. Sally Honer **made a motion to** hold a training seminar on March 15.
3. The treasurer **presented the latest report on** the FCBC's financial standing.
4. **Motion moved by** John H. Lee and **seconded by** Kimmy Walker.

### C  Closing
1. **Motion carried [failed].**
2. The members **were in agreement** and the **resolution was passed.**
3. February 26 and Conference Room 101 **were fixed as the time and place of the next meeting.**
4. **Meeting adjourned at** 1:40 p.m. **by** chair Julie Bouvier.

## 05 Mini Quiz

Fill in the blanks with the given words.

- was presided over by
- were in agreement
- made a motion to
- called the meeting to order

1. The members _____ and the resolution was passed.

2. The chairperson _____ at 9 a.m.

3. She _____ hold a training seminar on March 25.

4. The management meeting _____ Abigail Niehaus.

## 06 Email Writing (1)

Complete the minutes by writing the given words in each blank.

- hold
- seconded
- modification
- attendees
- standing
- order

Meeting of Board of Directors
Date: January 15, 2017
Place: Main Conference Room

(1)_____: David Holden (Chairperson), Adam Saad, Kimberly Ushiro, Kyle Baron
Absentees: (none)

I. Introduction
Meeting called to (2)_____ at 1:40 p.m. by chair David Holden.

II. Approval of minutes
Minutes from the meeting on January 8 approved without (3)_____.

III. Discussion
1. Finance Update
Treasurer Kimberly Ushiro presented the latest report on the FCBC's financial (4)_____.
2. Special Event
Kyle Baron made a motion to (5)_____ a training seminar on March 15.

IV. Conclusion
Motion: Motion moved by Kyle Baron and (6)_____ by Adam Saad.
Vote: 3 for, 1 opposed
Resolved: Motion carried

V. Closing
January 22 and the Main Conference Room were fixed as the time and place of the next meeting.
Meeting adjourned at 2:30 p.m. by chair David Holden.

# 07 Email Writing (2)

Fill in the blanks with your own information and complete the email below.

_____
             name of meeting

Date: _____
             commencement date

Place: _____
             designated meeting place

Attendees: _____(Chairperson), _____, _____, _____
      full name                  full name        full name        full name

Absentees: _____, _____
          full name        full name

### I. Introduction

Meeting called to order at _____ by _____.
                  commencement time        chairperson's name

### II. Approval of minutes

Minutes from the meeting on _____ approved without modification.
                  date of last meeting

### III. Discussion

1. _____
      action Item

   _____.
      explain the subject matter and the related team or person

2. _____
      other Item

   _____.
      explain the subject matter and the related team or person

### IV. Conclusion

Motion: _____ made a motion to _____ on _____.
         full name           content of proposal     date

Vote: _____ for, _____ opposed
      number for        number opposed

Resolved: Motion _____
              carried or rejected

### V. Closing

_____ and the _____ were fixed as the time
date of next meeting     designated meeting room

and place of the next meeting.

Meeting adjourned at _____ by _____.
             closing time      chairperson's name

## 08 Mr. Q's Email

Read the following and put yourself in Mr. Q's position. Then write an the minutes using the expressions you've learned.

> Mr. Q works on the marketing team at MQ Apparel and today he participated in a monthly marketing meeting as the minutes taker. The meeting was held at 10:00 a.m. in meeting room number 305. The attendees were Kelly Silver, Sammy Kim and Mr. Q himself. Mr. Harold Harris was absent. The chairperson was Kelly Silver. The meeting included discussions about last month's sales results and the sales promotion of the new Active Run Jacket.

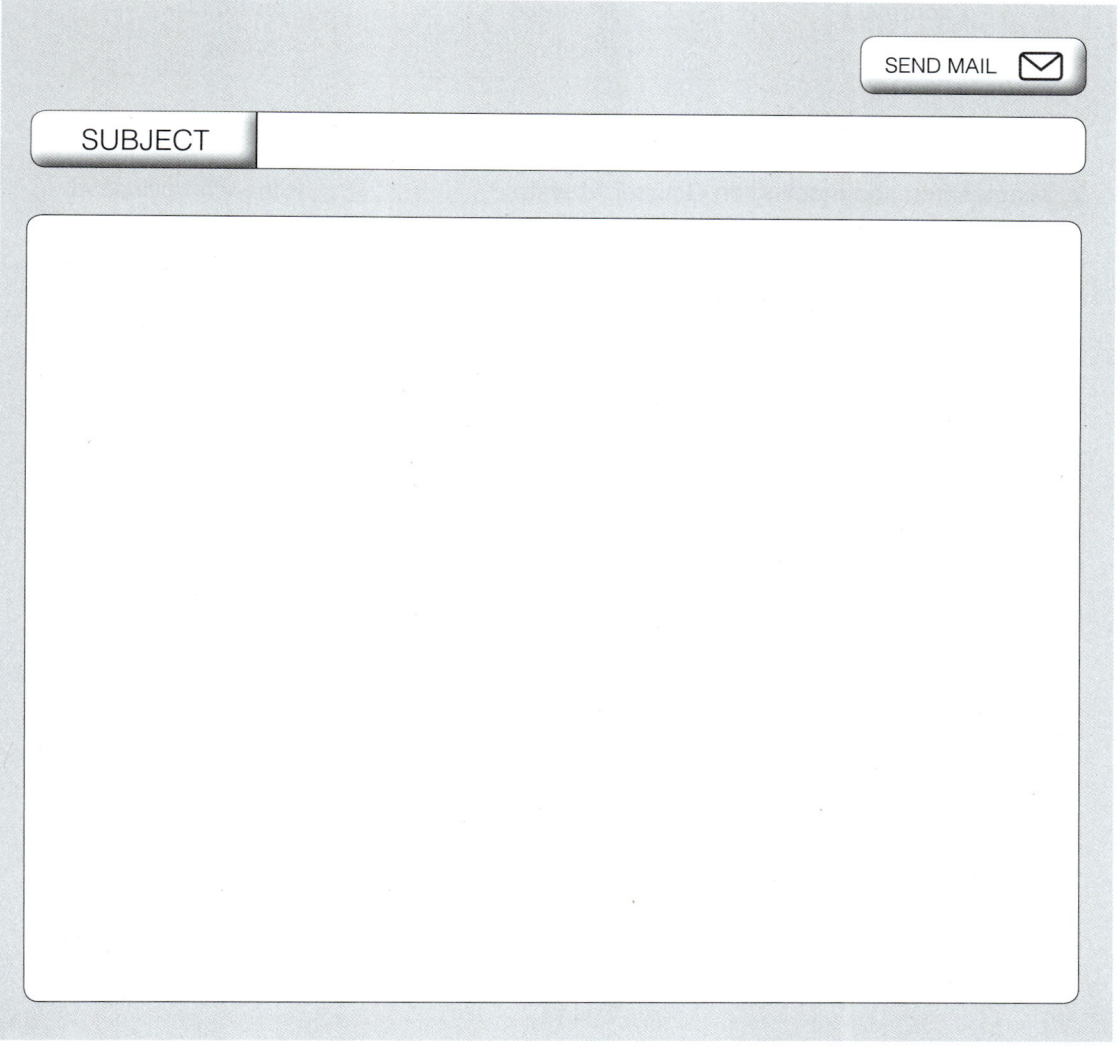

UNIT 14 Meeting Minutes

# 09 Exercise

**A  Underline the best word to complete each sentence.**

1  The chairperson called the meeting to (dismiss / order) at 10 a.m.

2  May 12 and Room 101 were (fixed / seconded) as the time and place of the next meeting.

**B  Fill in the blanks with the given words.**

- approved
- seconded
- presided
- agreement
- standing
- motion

1  The management meeting was _____ over by Heather Cino.

2  Minutes from the meeting on October 11 were _____ without modification.

3  The board members were in _____ and the proposal was passed.

4  We asked our manager to make a _____ to allocate more of the budget for marketing.

**C  Put the words in the right order.**

1  Chairman | presiding | convened | meeting | at 9:30 a.m | Alfredo Gomez

_____.

2  by | chair | adjourned | meeting | Jose Domingo | at 1:30 p.m.

_____.

3  standing | on | financial | presented | the FCBC's | the treasurer | the latest report

_____.

4  by | meeting | chair | called | Deby Davis | at 12:00 p.m. | to order

_____.

118  **BUSINESS INTERACTION** *E-mail*

# Unit 15

# Follow-up Email

## 01 Warm-up

1. In what cases do you need follow-up letters and how often do you write them?

2. Have you written a follow-up letter after an important meeting? What did you say in the letter and how did the recipient respond?

## 02 Writing Tips

1. Write a follow-up email right after the meeting/encounter with your business partner.

2. Thank the client for the opportunity to work with them.

3. Address concerns that your client might have or other important issues that need to be taken care of.

4. Highlight your company's key selling points and express confidence in meeting your client's needs.

5. Thank the client again and express interest in meeting them again soon.

# 03 Vocabulary

## A Word Definition
Underline the word with the given definition.

**1 to correct something that is wrong**

We are going to organize a special team to rectify the erroneous interpretations in the book.

**2 sure that something will happen in the way that you want or expect**

He is quietly confident that there will be no problems this time.

**3 a period or process in which business activity, production, etc is reduced and conditions become worse**

Were were facing a downturn in business, but we got through it because of your hard work.

**4 to show or prove that something is true**

How successful our business was over the past two years is attested to by these financial figures.

## B Word Use
Write your own sentence using the underlined word in the sentence.

1 Information must be translated into business **insight**.

_____

2 The unemployed population **drastically** dropped last year.

_____

3 Safety considerations override all other **concerns**.

_____

4 I am acutely **aware** of the difficulties we face.

_____

## 04 Expression

### A Thanking the recipient
1 **Thank you for taking the time to** meet with me yesterday.
2 **I just want to tell you how much** I appreciate you giving me the opportunity to present our offerings to you.
3 **It was a pleasure to** have the opportunity to receive your insight regarding the project.
4 **I very much appreciate you** taking time out of your busy schedule to address this matter.

### B Showing concern
1 **A similar project recently** went drastically over budget.
2 In that regard, **I understand your concerns about** the recent drops in stock prices.
3 We **are fully aware of** your situation and are doing our best to solve it as soon as we can.
4 **I'm positive that** our customer service will rectify this situation in short order.

### C Closing the email
1 I'm confident that our services **are a good fit for you.**
2 We appreciate **your enthusiastic response and feedback** to our offers.
3 **Good luck with your ventures,** and I hope to speak with you again in the near future.
4 I would like to thank you again **for taking the time out of your busy schedule.**

## 05 Mini Quiz

Fill in the blanks with the given words.

- I understand your concerns about
- are a good fit for you
- I'm positive that
- are fully aware of

1 We _____ what to do in case of an emergency.

2 _____ the situation in the car industry.

3 If you read this, you will know that we _____ as well as your needs.

4 _____ together we will achieve excellent results.

## 06 Email Writing (1)

Complete the email by writing the given words in each blank.

- rectify
- downturn
- opportunity
- reduction
- concerns
- ventures

Subject: Thank You for Yesterday's Meeting

Dear Ms. Christina Jones,

Thank you for taking the time to meet with me yesterday.

It was a pleasure to have the (1)_____ to get your insight regarding the Sun Valley project.

I understand your (2)_____ about the recent drops in stock prices. However, I'm positive that promising circumstances will (3)_____ this situation in short order.

Additionally, this (4)_____ in stock valuation, I would attest, can also be partly attributed to the recent (5)_____ in our industry as a whole.

Regardless of whether you think our services are a good fit for you, I would like to thank you again for taking the time out of your schedule.

Good luck with your (6)_____, and I hope to speak with you again in the near future.

Warm regards,

Nicole Durman
Project Supervisor
AccentU International Ltd.

# 07 Email Writing (2)

Fill in the blanks with your own information and complete the email below.

Subject: Our Recent Meeting

Dear _____,
       recipient's name

Thanks so much for taking the time to meet with me on _____.
                                                       date of the meeting.

It was great to finally discuss _____ with you. I understand
                                 matters that you discussed

your concerns about _____, though I'm positive that we can
                     your recipient's concerns

come up with a reasonable solution together.

Here is a case I've put together from a project similar to yours: _____
                                                                    link to case

Regardless of whether you think this is a good fit for you, I just want to tell you how much I appreciate the opportunity to talk with you.

Good luck with your ventures, and I hope to talk with you again soon.

Yours truly,

_____
   your full name

_____
   your job title

_____
   your company name

## 08  Mr. Q's Email

Read the following and put yourself in Mr. Q's position. Then write an email using the expressions you've learned.

> Mr. Q is a project supervisor at MQ Aerospace, a company that specializes in building telecommunications satellites. He recently had a very interesting meeting with Bob Mooney, an engineer who is working on the Ares IV space launch, and now Mr. Q would like to send him a short follow-up letter to thank him for his time.
>
> During their discussion, Mr. Mooney expressed concern about MQ Aerospace's first television satellite I which was made five years ago. The satellite is in poor condition, and is not expected to last more than another year or two. Regardless, Mr. Q assured him that his company is already working on some replacement parts that will permanently fix the satellite's problems.

SEND MAIL

SUBJECT

## 09 Exercise

**A** Underline the best word to complete each sentence.

1 We appreciate your (downturn / enthusiastic) response to our suggestion.

2 The recent M&A is (attributable / confident) to the company's current budget deficit.

**B** Fill in the blanks with the given words.

| • regardless | • rectified | • positive |
| • short | • attested | • aware |

1 I'm _____ that our products can be leading items with futher promotions.

2 The game will be held this weekend _____ of the weather.

3 Once you get back from the meeting, send them a follow-up email in _____ order.

4 How successful our business has been can be _____ to by the number of visitors per hour.

**C** Put the words in the right order.

1 a | drastically | recently | project | similar | went | over budget

_____.

2 I | in | the recent drops | understand | about | your concerns | stock prices

_____.

3 for | I'm | fit | that | you | are | a good | our services | confident

_____.

4 your | feedback | we | to | and | appreciate | our offers | enthusiastic response

_____.

126 BUSINESS INTERACTION E-mail

## Unit 16

# Executive Summary

## 01 Warm-up

1. What is the purpose of an executive summary and who is the intended target of your company's executive summary?

2. What are the short and long-term goals of your company? What would you like to emphasize when you write an executive summary to appeal to your prospective client?

## 02 Writing Tips

1. Demonstrate a clear understanding of the potential client/investor's needs.

2. Put the most critical information in the first couple of paragraphs.

3. You should not focus on what your plan is, but on what its return or benefits will be. For example, "This project will double current sales numbers."

4. Differentiate yourself-highlight a unique methodology, for instance, or provide a quick case study of your past work. Include testimonials from satisfied clients.

5. Use formatting and graphics to highlight your message.

## 03 Vocabulary

### A Word Definition
Underline the word with the given definition.

**1** made for or appealing to people who have a lot of money

Mulberry is taking its brand more upmarket from its traditional position.

**2** a feeling of wanting to do something

We have neither the time nor the inclination to work on other things.

**3** to acquire by effort; earn

The company has struggled to garner an appropriate share of the market.

**4** to produce or cause something

We are confident that we will generate up to $31,000 by the end of the year.

### B Word Use
Write your own sentence using the underlined word in the sentence.

**1** **Highlight** what your team members do right rather than wrong.

_____

**2** Comstar **secured** a $20 million contract.

_____

**3** Participants **contribute** to meetings in many ways.

_____

**4** They were trying to **expand** their business.

_____

## 04 Expression

**A Introducing a business plan**

1 **This business plan will highlight** our progress up until the day of the spa's launch.
2 We will **follow up with what our projection will look like** in the next five years.
3 **The purpose of the plan is** to secure funding and the finances necessary for the launching of Glo–Spa.
4 **Our long term aim is to** expand the line of treatments we offer.

**B Explaining target and parameters**

1 **Our target clients include** women between the ages of 20 and 60.
2 **Our edge lies in the fact that** we offer complete packages for all types of treatments.
3 Our location **is another great advantage.**

**C Referring to management and financial benefits**

1 The **management of Glo-Spa includes** co-owners Paul and Amy Johnstone who have 15 and 20 years, respectively, of experience in the industry.
2 In addition, we **expect to triple our sales** by the end of the year.
3 The planned location and target clientele **should contribute to $50,000 in revenue in** the first quarter.

## 05 Mini Quiz

Fill in the blanks with the given words.

- the purpose of the plan is to
- our target clients include
- we expect to double our sales
- our long term aim is to

1 _____ improve the company's profitability.

2 _____ provide direction and guidance for the management of outdoor recreation resources in the area.

3 _____ major corporate marketers, retail chains, creative agencies, entertainment production, architects and graphic design companies.

4 _____ from 24,000 units to 50,000 units by December of this year.

## 06 Email Writing (1)

Complete the email by writing the given words in each blank.

- expand
- advantage
- purpose
- target
- upmarket
- figures

Subject: Glo-Spa Executive Summary

Glo-Spa is a new (1) _____ day spa located in Boston, Massachusetts. We have specialists who are well versed and trained in over twenty different styles of massages and treatments. We also offer a full hair and beauty salon on the premises.

The (2) _____ of the plan is to secure the funding and finances necessary for a great launch.

Our (3) _____ clients include women between the ages of 20 and 60 who have the means and the inclination to try out the services we provide.

Our edge lies in the fact that we offer a complete package for all types of treatments, from head to toe.

Our location is another (4) _____ as the spa is to be located near four upmarket residential neighborhoods. Our long term aim is to (5) _____ the line of treatments we offer to match up with changes in the industry and also to transform our spa into a popular vacation destination.

The management of Glo-Spa includes co-owners, Celia Nox and Alise Fowler, both of whom have 15 and 20 years, respectively, of experience in the industry.

Based on the size of the market area and the target client, we expect to garner sales of almost USD $50,000 by the first quarter. In addition, we expect to triple these (6) _____ by the end of the year.

# 07 Email Writing (2)

Fill in there are no blanks your own information and complete the email below.

Subject: Executive Summary of Glo-Spa

| | |
|---|---|
| **Introduction** | Introduce your company, its history, achievements, structure and location. |
| **Services/Products** | Write a description of the products or services your company provides. |
| **Target Group** | Explain who your intended target audience is and how your products and services are suitable for them |
| **Differentiating Factor** | Describe the edge that your company has over its competitors. This is to attract prospective financiers and investors. |
| **Objective** | Mention the goals your company has set for itself in the short and long term. |
| **Business Management** | Mention the members of your management team. It is important to highlight what experience they have in your company's field. |
| **Financial Details** | Note the sales projections for the current year and the sales of past years. It would also be a good idea to include any investment plans that you have in mind for your business. |

## 08 Mr. Q's Email

Read the following and put yourself in Mr. Q's position. Then write an email using the expressions you've learned.

> Mr. Q, who is starting his own business, MQ Bicycles, in Atlanta, Georgia, needs to write an email to solicit investment. He has 15 years' experience working in the fields of bicycle repair and sales, and is a five-time gold-medal winning BMX racer. MQ Bicycles will build and sell bicycles for all ages and purposes, from tricycles for children to multiple-gear mountain bikes. Mr. Q believes his fame as a racer will provide him the edge he needs to become successful. Also, the location of his shop being in the close vicinity of a popular bicycle trail should help boost sales. He is confident that MQ Bicycles will generate up to $25,000 by the end of the first quarter, and should quadruple that by the end of the year.

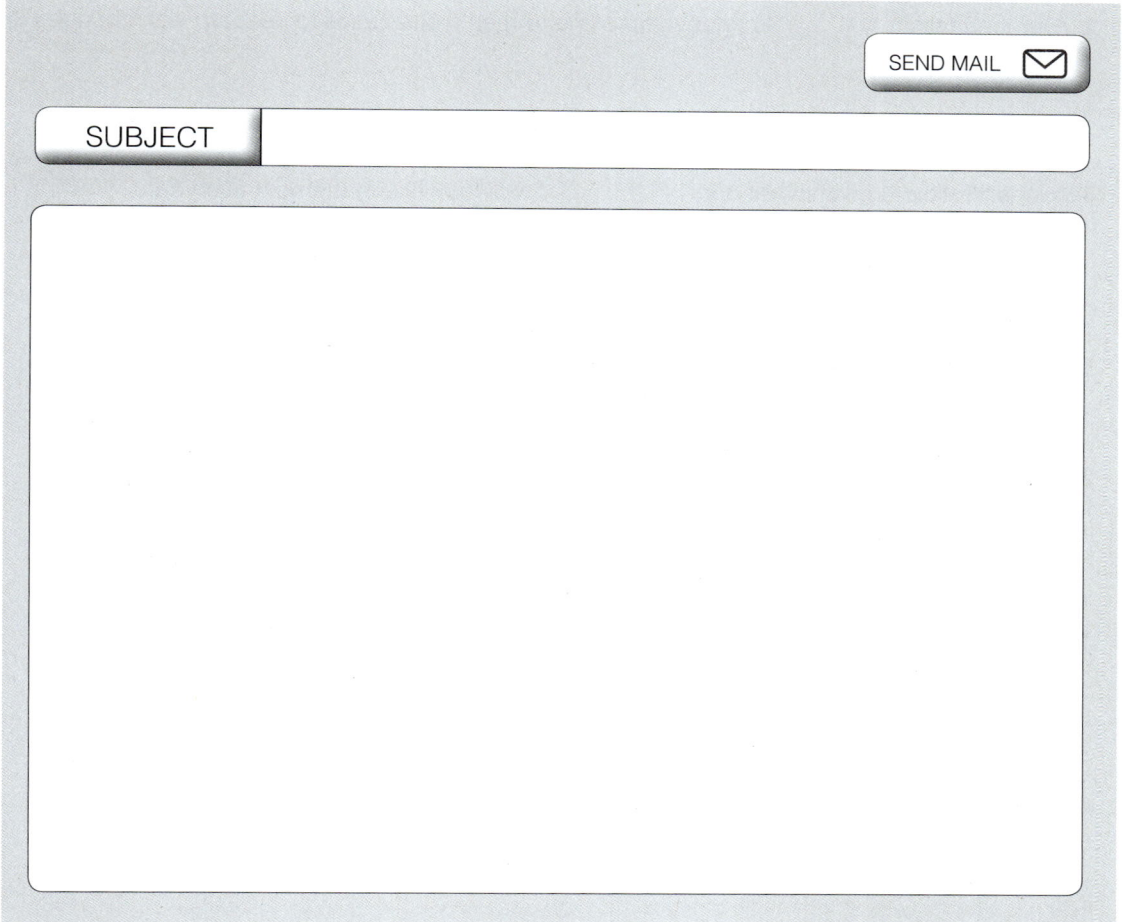

## 09 Exercise

**A  Underline the best word to complete each sentence.**

1. Our target clients (include / require) teenagers in the age group of 17 to 19 who get stressed from studying.
2. Israeli firms (enrich / generate) $12 billion in business in Massachusetts.

**B  Fill in the blanks with the given words.**

- edge
- aim
- contribute
- projection
- triple
- confident

1. We expect to _____ our sales by the end of the third quarter.
2. Our long term _____ is to develop a line of men's cosmetics to keep up with changes in the industry.
3. Our _____ lies in the fact that we offer a customized package.
4. We will follow up with what our _____ will look like in the next five years.

**C  Put the words in the right order.**

1. owners | small and medium | we're | business | targeting

   _____.

2. of | until | our progress | the day | this business plan | highlight | will | up | the spa's | launch

   _____.

3. of | is | for | to secure | the launching | necessary | the purpose | the plan | funding and | the finances | of Glo-spa

   _____.

4. up to | by | of | confident | we | that | are | we will generate | $25,000 | the end | the first | quarter

   _____.

# Unit 17

# Notifying Contract Termination

## 01 Warm-up

1. Did any of your clients violate a contract and create a serious problem? Are there any terms that your company values the most when writing a contract?

2. Have you heard of any contract termination agreement cases? What caused it and how did the company respond?

## 02 Writing Tips

1. Maintain a polite tone and use some form of greeting before the body of the letter.

2. Explain the reason for the termination thoroughly, so that there is no misunderstanding.

3. Do not go into too many details, as it is best to stick to the facts and keep it simple when possible.

## 03 Vocabulary

### A Word Definition
Underline the word with the given definition.

**1** a part of a written law or legal document covering a particular subject of the whole law or document

The contract contains 14 **clauses** to which both parties finally agreed.

**2** to disobey or do something against an official agreement, law, or principle

The court denied Samsung's claim that Apple **violated** three of its patents.

**3** to bring something to an end

The company decided to **terminate** its original plan to reduce its number of offices.

**4** spoken rather than written

Strong **verbal** skills will help to enliven discussion.

### B Word Use
Write your own sentence using the underlined word in the sentence.

**1** Each country has different social **norms**.

_____

**2** At the weekly meeting, the manager announced **drastic** changes to the whole intranet structure.

_____

**3** That manufacturer imitates the designs of a **competitor**.

_____

**4** We hope that this arrangement is **satisfactory** to you.

_____

## 04 Expression

### A  Referring to violated clauses

1  Your company **was found to be in violation of clause** 49, which deals with corporate governance norms.
2  **Your company violated clause** 24 which says that your company cannot work with a third party while continuing to work with us.
3  **The reason behind this drastic measure** is that your company violated Clause 19 of our contract by making a deal with one of our competitors.

### B  Introducing your company

1  Despite numerous warnings, your company was still **found to be violating** our contract clauses.
2  **We have previously given you both verbal and written warnings** of these violations.
3  While we have tried to allow for a satisfactory resolution to this matter, **our patience has unfortunately worn too thin to proceed further.**

### C  Introducing your products

1  **Hence, we had no option but to terminate** our contract.
2  **This leaves us no choice but to terminate the agreement with you as of** June 19 and move on to another contractor.
3  Kindly get in touch with him as soon as possible **to bring about a final resolution to this matter.**

## 05 Mini Quiz

Fill in the blanks with the given words.

- found to be in violation of
- leaves us no choice but to
- bring about a final resolution to
- reserves the right to terminate

1  NP _____ contracts if contractors fail to meet their obligations.

2  Their refusal _____ take legal action.

3  SRT was _____ a number of safety regulations.

4  In order to _____ all matters in dispute, a settlement has been agreed upon.

## 06 Email Writing (1)

Complete the email by writing the given words in each blank.

- option
- unfortunate
- continuing
- communicate
- measure
- satisfactory

Subject: Contract Termination

Dear Ms. Stephanie Brisbane,

This is to inform your company that the contract between us has been terminated as of December 11. The reason behind taking this drastic (1)_____ is that your company violated Clause 19 of our contract by making a deal with one of our competitors. You also violated Clause 24 which says that your company cannot work with a third party while (2)_____ to work with us.

While we have tried to be patient and allow for a (3)_____ resolution to this matter, our patience has unfortunately worn too thin to proceed further.
Despite numerous warnings, your company was still found to be violating our contract clauses. Hence, we had no (4)_____ but to terminate our contract.

Please (5)_____ with Mr. Oliver Heinze who will explain in detail the required paperwork for you to receive your final payment.

Although we consider this contract termination to be an (6)_____ but necessary option, we wish you luck in the future and thank you for your services.

Regards,

Dmitri Popov
Sales Manager
Ryan Co.

# 07 Email Writing (2)

Fill in the blanks with your own information and complete the email below.

Subject: Contract Termination

Dear _____,
　　　　　receiver's name

This is to inform you that the _____ between us has been
　　　　　　　　　　　　　　　　　　name or type of the contract

terminated as of _____ We regret to take this action, but we
　　　　　　　　　the date of contract termination

had no other options. The reason behind this drastic measure is that your company violated

_____ of our contract by _____.
the contract clause number that was violated　　　　　explain the clause the receiver violated

Your company also violated _____ which says that
　　　　　　　　　　　　　additional violated contract clause number

_____. This was despite the warnings we gave you earlier.
explain the clause the receiver violated

_____.
mention any more details regarding the violations

Hence, we had no option but to terminate our contract.

Please make sure to meet _____, who will explain in
　　　　　　　　　　　　name of the person in charge of the termination

detail the required paperwork necessary to get your final payment. Kindly get in touch with

him/her. We wish you luck in your future and would like to thank you for working with us.

Best regards,

_____
　　　　your full name

_____
　　　　your job title

_____
　　　your company name

## 08 Mr. Q's Email

Read the following and put yourself in Mr. Q's position. Then write an email using the expressions you've learned.

> Mr. Q is the sales manager for MQ Foods, a supermarket franchise in North Carolina.
> One of MQ Foods' major suppliers, Sun Tree Produce, has breached their sales contract too many times, so Mr. Q has to write a letter to Warren Chartrain, general manager of Sun Tree Produce, to inform him that MQ Foods is terminating the contract between the two companies as of June 19, 2018. The clauses that Sun Tree Produce violated were:
> Clause 17, by failing to arrange transportation as agreed and Clause 26, by breaking deliveries into multiple shipments without prior agreement. The contract had been violated a total of five times.

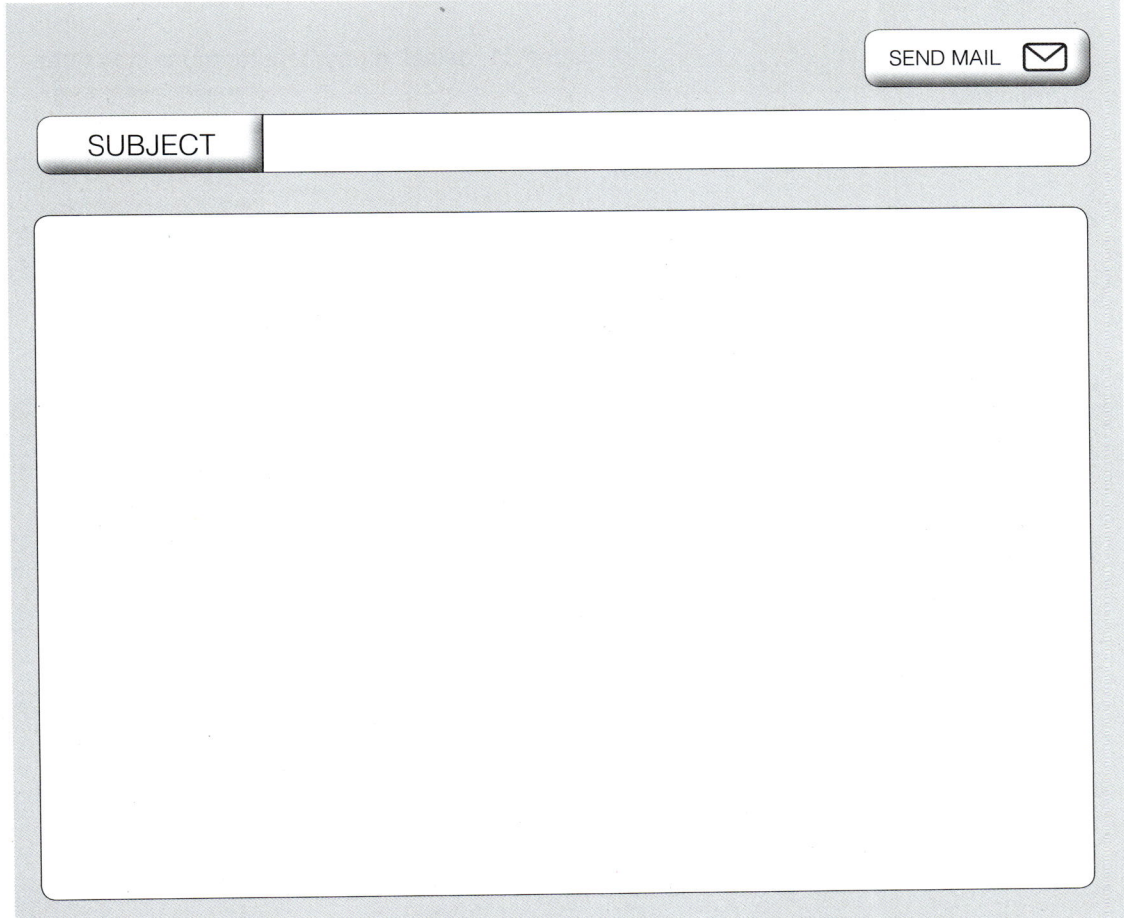

## 09 Exercise

**A** Underline the best word to complete each sentence.

1 Hence, we had no option but to (terminate / fertilize) our contract.

2 Despite (numeric / numerous) warnings, your company was still found to be violating our contract clauses.

**B** Fill in the blanks with the given words.

- inclined
- verbal
- resolution
- norms
- drastic
- violation

1 _____ measures are being taken by the city council to upgrade their infrastructure.

2 Your company is in _____ of clause 21, delaying payment for more than three months.

3 We already gave both _____ and written warnings of these violations.

4 Although we warned you not to use those materials, you were still _____ to do so.

**C** Put the words in the right order.

1 thin | has | worn | our | patience | this contract | too | to keep

_____ .

2 a | contact | final | to bring about | please | resolution | him | to this matter

_____ .

3 prior | we | notice | without | to terminate | the right | reserve | the contract

_____ .

4 in detail | for you | Mr. Kim | to receive | final payment | will | your | explain | the required | paperwork

_____ .

# Unit 18

# Memorandum of Understanding

## 01 Warm-up

1. Have you ever struggled to understand a memorandum of understanding to resolve the problem? What did you do?

2. A memorandum of understanding agreement is a non-binding agreement. What would you do if you found out your partner had violated the agreement?

## 02 Writing Tips

1. Determine what functions, services, or resources will be provided by one party to the other. You may also discuss a plan that details how the parties will operate together.

2. List all of the parties involved and write out the main purpose of the agreement. Detail the specific outcomes that are expected.

3. Determine a timeline as to when the partnership will begin and when it will end. Be specific and note the dates in the memorandum of understanding (MOU).

4. Write down which organizations will be responsible for the different services and resources. Detail how the MOU can be terminated.

5. Allow all of the parties to review, sign and authorize the MOU. Include the contact information of all parties.

## 03 Vocabulary

### A Word Definition
Underline the word with the given definition.

1  a process in which you make a judgment about a person or situation
   We all agreed on the assessment the boss made of the new recruit.

2  an event or state of affairs that is required before something else will occur
   I don't think the conditions precedent of the contract are fair.

3  the care that a reasonable person exercises to avoid harm to other persons or their property
   The corporation conducts due diligence every May, according to their agreement.

4  to begin or to start something
   The meeting is scheduled to commence at noon.

### B Word Use
Write your own sentence using the underlined word in the sentence.

1  The cost of building is **estimated** at 500 million won.
   _____

2  The company has a one-year **exclusivity** deal on the software with Sun Motor Co.
   _____

3  Their refusal to pay is a **breach** of the contract.
   _____

4  The deal is currently set to **expire** two years from now.
   _____

## 04 Expression

### A  Referring to the parties involved
1  KESCO and OMICRON **conclude the Memorandum of Understanding as below.**
2  As per the MOU, **a contract of sale shall be executed between the parties.**
3  A Memorandum of Understanding **was signed between** Desert Sun **and** Alpaca Traders **in connection with** the sale of Alpaca's rights.

### B  Referring to the terms of the MOU
1  According to Desert Sun's assessment, **the total consideration for the sale of** Alpaca's rights **is estimated at a range of** USD 105-120 million.
2  The consideration amount and the consideration adjustment mechanisms **are set forth in the MOU.**
3  It was agreed between the parties that the transaction **will be subject to the fulfillment of various conditions precedent.**

### C  Referring to the time period
1  During the exclusivity period, the Foreign Corporation **shall conduct a due diligence.**
2  Alpaca **granted** the Foreign Corporation **the option to extend the exclusivity period for** an additional 30 days, under certain conditions.
3  **During the duration of this agreement, all parties agree to** act in good faith and to notify all other parties of an anticipated breach of any terms.

## 05 Mini Quiz

Fill in the blanks with the given words.

- in connection with
- is set forth
- be subject to the fulfillment of
- be hereinafter referred to as

1  The consideration amount _____ on the last page of the contract.

2  The transaction will _____ various conditions precedent.

3  Boston Community College will _____ "BCU."

4  An MOU was signed between Goden Inc. and Sam Cycle _____ the sale of Sam Cycle's rights.

## 06 Email Writing (1)

Complete the memorandum by writing the given words in each blank.

- precedent
- subject
- according
- connection
- conduct
- transaction

Memorandum of Understanding of Subsidiary

In accordance with the report provided to the Company by James Locker January 12 the Company hereby reports the following:

1. In accordance with the report provided to the Company by Desert Sun Wholesale, the Company hereby reports the sale of Alpaca's rights as contained in the "MOU" sales contract between the parties (1)_____ to Desert Sun's assessment. On July 8 a Memorandum of Understanding was signed between Desert Sun Wholesale and Alpaca Traders Ltd. in (2)_____ with the sale of Alpaca's rights.

2. It was agreed between the parties that the (3)_____ will be subject, inter alia, to the fulfillment of various conditions (4)_____.

3. Simultaneously with the execution of the MOU, an exclusivity agreement was signed between the parties according to which, (5)_____ to certain conditions, during the period ending on August 9, 2017, Alpaca will not be entitled to conduct contacts with third parties for the sale of its rights. Furthermore, Alpaca granted Desert Sun an option to extend the exclusivity period for an additional 30 days, under certain conditions during the exclusivity period Desert Sun shall (6)_____ a due diligence.

UNIT 18 Memorandum of Understanding

# 07 Email Writing (2)

Fill in the blanks with your own information and complete the memorandum below.

Memorandum of Understanding

1. On _____, a non-binding Memorandum of Understanding
           *date the memorandum was signed*

   was signed between _____ and _____
                         *name of first signee*              *reason for memorandum*

   in connection with reason for memorandum.

2. It was agreed between the parties that the transaction will be subject, inter alia, to the fulfillment of various conditions precedent.

3. An exclusivity agreement which was signed between the parties is subject to certain conditions during the period ending on last date of exclusivity agreement. state the reason for the exclusivity agreement. Furthermore, the Foreign Corporation was granted an option to extend the exclusivity period for additional duration of possible extension, under certain conditions. During the exclusivity period, the Foreign Corporation shall conduct a due diligence.

## 08 Mr. Q's Email

Read the following and put yourself in Mr. Q's position. Then write a memorandum using the expressions you've learned.

Mr. Q is the owner of MQ Instruments, a musical instrument store. He is to sign a memorandum of understanding with the owner of Harpy Guitars, a guitar production company. The MOU will be a non-binding agreement effective once production of the new Harpy guitar line begins. MQ Instruments will purchase the guitars at an estimated cost of $320 each, for distribution and sale. The MOU will be signed on March 27 and includes an exclusivity agreement ending on March 26 that Harpy must not sell their guitars to any other music store for a period of one year. There is an option for MQ Instruments to extend the exclusivity agreement for 60 more days under certain conditions.

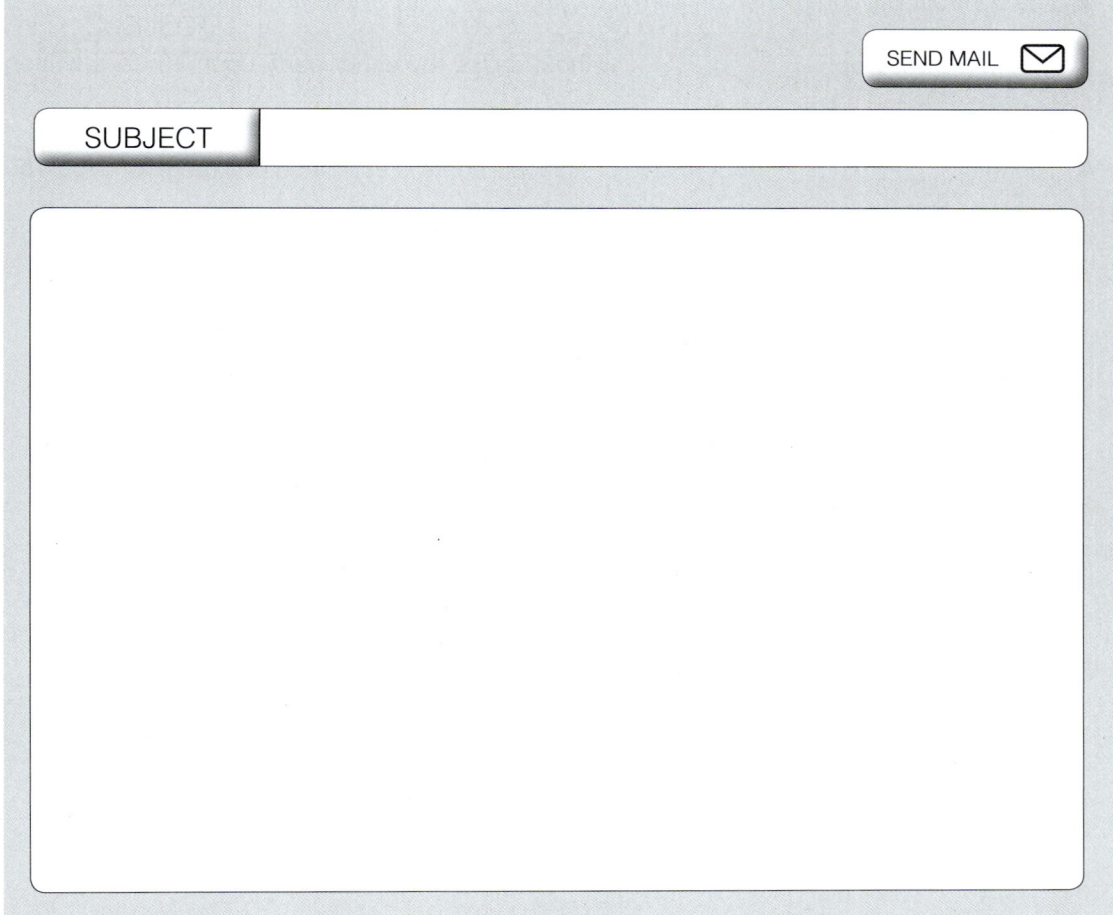

UNIT 18 Memorandum of Understanding

## 09 Exercise

**A  Underline the best word to complete each sentence.**

1  ATRN and BCL (conclude / exclude) the Memorandum of Understanding as below.

2  All parties agree to act in good faith and to notify all other parties of an (anticipant / anticipated) breach of any of its terms.

**B  Fill in the blanks with the given words.**

- terminated
- duration
- due diligence
- consideration
- expire
- referred

1  During the exclusivity period, a _____ will be conducted.

2  The contract will commence on March 27 and _____ after a year on March 26.

3  This MOU may be _____, without cause, by either party upon 15 days written notice.

4  The total _____ for the sale of Alpaca's rights is estimated at a range of $100-150 million.

**C  Put the words in the right order.**

1  be executed | a contract of sale | between | as per | the MOU | shall | the parties

_____.

2  the fulfillment | will | of | precedent | the transaction | conditions | be subject to | various

_____.

3  the MOU | set | amount | forth | the consideration | is | in

_____.

4  the exclusivity | Alpaca granted | period | an additional 30 days | the option | for | the Foreign Corporation | to extend | under certain conditions

_____.

# Unit 19

## Sales Contract

## 01 Warm-up

1 Have you ever been in trouble because of a misunderstanding or miscommunication regarding a contract for a sale of goods?

2 What is the most important thing when you create a contract for a sale of goods? What would you do if there were a term that you could not accept?

## 02 Writing Tips

1 Clearly indicate dates specifying when the contract will begin and expire.

2 Neatly specify the goods or services in question and the prices that were agreed upon.

3 The sale of goods or services involves guaranteeing quality and satisfaction to the buyer. It may be useful to mention what "satisfactory quality" or "fit for purpose" would actually mean in terms of goods or services that would be provided.

4 Include a schedule for the delivery of goods or services, shipping charges, and warranty.

5 Ensure legal enforceability of the contract.

## 03 Vocabulary

### A  Word Definition
Underline the word with the given definition.

1  **not able to be changed, reversed, or recovered; final**
The decision will not be irrevocable until everyone concerned has been consulted.

2  **dealing with things that are important or real**
We need more substantive reasons in order to break the current contract.

3  **skill in making things, especially in a way that makes them look good**
Swiss watches are known for their precision workmanship.

4  **a tax on goods coming into a country or going out of a country**
Tariff cuts typically increases foreign trade volume.

### B  Word Use
Write your own sentence using the underlined word in the sentence.

1  The Buyer **warrants** that they provide the letter of credit as a payment method issued in compliance with applicable law.

_____

2  The **carrier** was finally selected in consideration of its reasonable delivery charges.

_____

3  All **casualties** to the goods in transit shall be the responsibility of the Seller.

_____

4  Your manufacturing department should be **liable** for any defective products.

_____

## 04 Expression

### A  Referring to delivery and risk of loss
1  **Buyer will give Seller 30 days' advance notice regarding** the quantity requested for delivery.
2  Upon receipt of the request for delivery, **Seller will arrange for delivery through a** carrier chosen by Seller, the costs of which shall be F.O.B.
3  **The risk of loss** from any casualty to the goods, **regardless of the cause, will be the responsibility** of the Buyer once the goods have been shipped by the Seller.

### B  Referring to acceptance
1  Buyer shall **have the right to inspect the goods upon receipt.**
2  Buyer must **give notice to Seller of any claim for damages** on account of condition, quality, or grade of the goods within two business days after delivery.

### C  Referring to warranties and taxes
1  **Seller warrants that the goods sold hereunder are new and free from** substantive defects in workmanship and materials.
2  **Seller's liability under the foregoing warranty is limited to** the replacement of goods or refund of the purchase price at Seller's sole option.
3  **Seller gives 14 days of limited warranty unless otherwise specified, from the date of delivery.**

## 05 Mini Quiz

Fill in the blanks with the given words.

> · under the foregoing warranty is limited to
> · to inspect the goods upon
> · give Seller 30 days' advance notice regarding
> · be the responsibility of

1  The risk of loss from any damages to the goods will _____ the Buyer once the goods have been shipped by the Seller.

2  Buyer shall have the right _____ receipt.

3  Buyer will _____ the quantity requested for delivery.

4  Seller's liability _____ the replacement of goods or refund of the purchase price at Seller's sole option.

## 06 Email Writing (1)

Complete the contract by writing the given words in each blank.

- account
- otherwise
- acceptance
- responsibility
- receipt
- hereunder

This Contract for Sale of Goods is made on November 20 by and between Desert Sun Wholesale ("Seller" with its principal place of business at 6115 La Vista Dr., Dallas, TX, and Supershop ("Buyer" with its principal place of business at 9201, W. Sunset Blvd, Los Angeles, CA, for the purchase of the goods described below:

| Quantity | Item No. | Description | Price | Total |
|---|---|---|---|---|
| 200 | AR430 | Kitchen Pro stainless 8-inch open skillet | $6.12 | $1,224.00 |
| 150 | AR199 | Kitchen Pro 14-inch cast iron wok | $13.99 | $2,098.50 |
| | | | TOTAL | $3,322.50 |

1. Terms. This Contract shall begin on November 20, and end upon the last delivery for the quantity specified in this agreement, unless the parties agree (1)_____.

2. Delivery. Buyer will give Seller 30 days' advance notice regarding the quantity requested for delivery. Upon (2)_____ of the request for delivery, Seller will arrange for delivery through a carrier chosen by Seller, the costs of which shall be F.O.B.

3. Risk of Loss. The risk of loss from any casualty to the Goods will be the (3)_____ of the Buyer once the goods have been shipped by the Seller.

4. Acceptance. Buyer will have the right to inspect the goods upon receipt. Within two business days after delivery, Buyer must give notice to Seller of any claim for damages on

   (4)_____ account of condition, quality, or grade of the goods. Failure of Buyer to give notice of damaged goods will constitute irrevocable (5)_____ of the goods by Buyer.

5. Charges. Seller shall invoice Buyer upon and for each shipment. Buyer shall pay all charges within 30 days of the receipt of goods. Overdue invoices shall also bear interest at the rate of 2% per month.

6. Warranty. Seller warrants that the goods sold (6)_____ are new and free from substantive defects in workmanship and materials. Seller's liability under the foregoing warranty is limited to the replacement of goods or refund of the purchase price at Seller's sole option.

7. Taxes. All sales taxes, tariffs, and other governmental charges shall be paid by Buyer and are Buyer's responsibility except as limited by the law.

## 07 Email Writing (2)

Fill in no blanks exist below, fix formatting your own information and complete the contract below.

Sales Contract for _____
                    name of product

This Contract for Sale of Goods is made this _____ by and between
                                              date of agreement

_____ ("Seller" with its principal place of business at _____,)
    name of seller                                                          location

and _____ ("Buyer" with its principal place of business at _____,
      name of buyer                                                           location

for the purchase of the goods described below:

| Quantity | Item number | Description | Price | Total |
|----------|-------------|-------------|-------|-------|
|          |             |             |       |       |
|          |             |             |       |       |
|          |             |             |       |       |

1. Terms. This Contract shall begin on _____ and end upon the last
                                        number of days
   delivery of the quantity specified in this agreement, unless the parties agree otherwise.

2. Delivery. Buyer will give Seller _____ days' advance notice regarding
                                      beginning date
   the quantity requested for delivery. Upon receipt of the request for delivery, Seller will arrange
   for delivery through a carrier chosen by Seller, the costs of which shall be F.O.B.

3. Risk of Loss. The risk of loss from any damage to the goods, regardless of the cause, will be the
   responsibility of the Buyer once the goods have been shipped by the Seller.

4. Acceptance. Buyer will have the right to inspect the goods upon receipt, and within two
   business days after delivery, Buyer must give notice to Seller of any claim for damages on
   account of condition, quality, or grade of the goods.

5. Charges. Seller shall invoice Buyer upon and for each shipment. Buyer shall pay all charges
   within _____ days of the receipt of goods.
           number of days

6. Warranty. Seller warrants that the goods sold hereunder are new and free from substantive
   defects in workmanship and materials.

7. Taxes. All sales taxes, tariffs, and other governmental charges shall be paid by Buyer and are
   Buyer's responsibility except as limited by the law.

## 08 Mr. Q's Email

Read the following and put yourself in Mr. Q's position. Then write a contract using the expressions you've learned.

Mr. Q is the purchasing manager for MQ Foods, and he needs to fill out a new contract with Sun Tree Produce to place a purchase order for the following items: 150 bags of Sun Frozen Mixed Vegetables (Item Number AP436, $2.99 per bag, $488.50 total); 100 boxes of Sun Plain Yogurt 4-packs (Item Number AP277, $2.20 per box, $220.00 total); and 175 boxes of Sun Crackers (Item Number AP101, $0.90 per box, $157.50 total). The total price for the entire order is $866.00. The contract will begin on January 10, which is 30 days from now. Also, Sun Tree Produce charges a 4% interest penalty to overdue invoices.

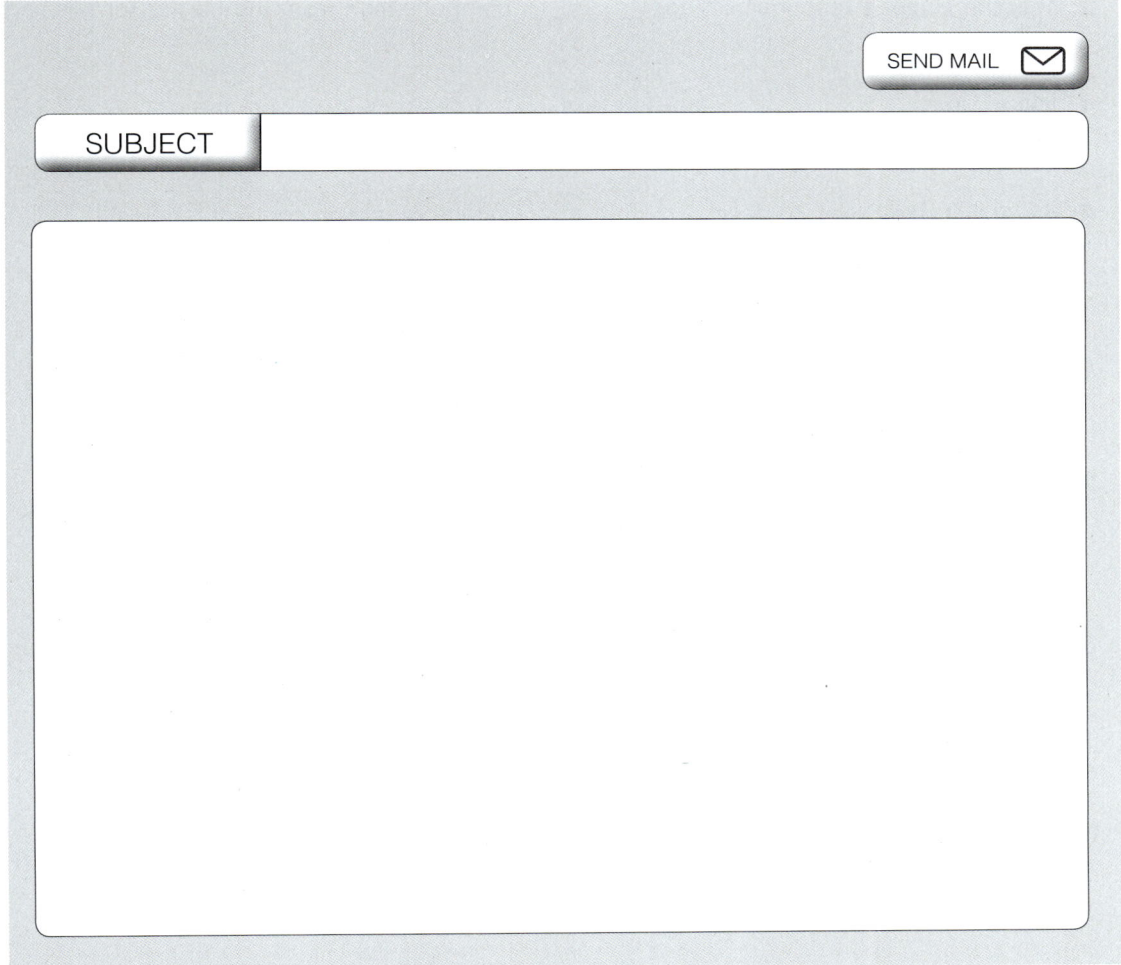

## 09 Exercise

### A  Underline the best word to complete each sentence.

1  Buyer shall have the right to (inspect / inspire) the goods upon receipt.

2  Buyer must (speculate / specify) the basis of the claim in detail.

### B  Fill in the blanks with the given words.

- liability
- carrier
- advance
- warranty
- seek
- casualties

1  All _____ to the products in transit shall be the responsibility of the Seller.

2  It is the Buyer's responsibility to _____ compensation from the carrier for missing freight.

3  The Seller's _____ under the foregoing warranty is limited to the replacement of goods.

4  Buyer will give Seller 30 days' _____ notice regarding contract renewal.

### C  Put the words in the right order.

1  chosen | will | a carrier | delivery | Seller | through | by Seller | arrange for

_____.

2  free | defects | the goods | are | from | Seller | substantive | warrants that | sold | hereunder

_____.

3  of | will | acceptance | irrevocable | constitute | of damaged goods | Failure of Buyer | by | Buyer | to give notice | the goods

_____.

4  otherwise specified | of limited warranty | from the date | 14 days | Seller | gives | unless | of delivery

_____.

158  BUSINESS INTERACTION  *E-mail*

## Unit 20

## Thank You Email

## 01 Warm-up

1. Have you ever received an appreciation letter from your client or business partner? What was the occasion and what did they say?

2. Do you have any clients who are very memorable? What is the reason and what would you like to mention if you were to write an letter of appreciation to them?

## 02 Writing Tips

1. Explain why you are showing your thanks. Mention specific reasons.

2. Be direct and concise in your writing.

3. Wish them luck in their future endeavors.

4. Show anticipation of working with them in the near future.

5. Only thank someone for something already done; to thank in advance is presumptuous.

# 03 Vocabulary

## A  Word Definition
Underline the word with the given definition.

**1**  able to be trusted to do what you need or expect

We would like to thank you for dependable technical support since we started working together.

**2**  producing a profit or a useful result

In order to build a profitable business, you need to offer something that others are looking for.

**3**  respected and admired

She was a good conductor, and was highly esteemed by the company.

**4**  the feeling that you can trust someone or something to be good, work well, or produce good results

Customers had the utmost confidence in the merchandise quality.

## B  Word Use
Write your own sentence using the underlined word in the sentence.

**1**  Local retail shops and restaurants benefit from the **thriving** tourism in the area.

_____

**2**  I am looking forward to making a **long-lasting** and successful partnership with you.

_____

**3**  They finally reached a satisfying conclusion for all **concerned** after two weeks of difficult negotiations.

_____

**4**  They opened a **magnificent** park landscaped by Future Landscaping.

_____

## 04 Expression

### A  Thanking for patronage

1  **Let me take this opportunity to thank you for choosing** BestBlue Kitchen Utensils.
2  As the year draws to a close, we wanted to **let you know how much we appreciate your continued patronage.**
3  **I appreciate all your help in** getting our store ready for the grand opening.
4  We recognize that our success **is made possible by partners such as you.**

### B  Sharing satisfaction for being a partner

1  **You have been a loyal and dependable business partner** over the past several years.
2  **We share in your satisfaction of watching your company grow** from a new venture into a thriving organization.
3  We are **pleased that you have made** our hand and body soaps **your premier choice.**
4  **Your experience and skills in** interior design made a difference in the reopening.

### C  Displaying future expectations as a partner

1  **We welcome the opportunity to** continue to assist you in meeting your goals.
2  I am very appreciative of your assistance and **wish you continued success in the future.**
3  **We look forward to a long-lasting relationship** which will be profitable and satisfying for all concerned.


## 05 Mini Quiz

Fill in the blanks with the given words.

- look forward to a long-lasting relationship
- is made possible by
- welcome the opportunity to
- have been a dependable partner

1  You _____ over the past several years.

2  We truly believe that our success _____ partners such as you.

3  We _____ which will be profitable and satisfying for all concerned.

4  We _____ continue to assist you in meeting your goals.

## 06 Email Writing (1)

Complete the email by writing the given words in each blank.

- premier
- satisfying
- ability
- thriving
- patronage
- meeting

Subject: Thank you for your continued patronage

Dear Ms. Kelly Paulson,

Thank you for your confidence in our (1)_____ to serve you. As December draws to a close and we look back at the year we have had, we feel we should remind you of how much

we appreciate your continued (2)_____ and enjoy having your organization as one of our esteemed supporters. While Best Washes is proud to be a leading provider of beauty soap, we recognize that our success is also made possible by partners such as you.

We understand that you have many options in the marketplace, and are pleased that you

have made our hand and body soaps your (3)_____ choice. You have been a loyal and dependable business partner over the past several years We share in your satisfaction

of watching your company grow from a new venture into a (4)_____ and dynamic organization.

We welcome the opportunity to continue to assist you in (5)_____ your goals and look

forward to a long-lasting relationship which will be profitable and (6)_____ for all concerned.

If at any time you have any questions or concerns, please do not hesitate to contact me or any member of our support staff.

Best regards,

Albert Cox
Sales Manager
Best Washes LTD.

UNIT 20 Thank You Email

## 07 Email Writing (2)

Fill in the blanks with your own information and complete the email below.

Subject: Thank you for being our valued client

Dear _____,
          customer name

Thank you for your confidence in our ability to serve you. As the year draws to a close, we wanted to let you know how much we appreciate your continued patronage.

_____ is proud to be a leading provider of _____.
   your company's name                                                       product / service

We understand that you have many options in the marketplace, and are pleased that you have made _____ your premier choice. You have been a loyal and
                    your company's name

dependable client for the past several years. We have watched your company grow from a brand new business to a thriving establishment.

We welcome the opportunity to assist you in your business and look forward to a continuing relationship which will be profitable for all concerned.

We are pleased to have you as our client, and wish you continued success.

Best regards,

_____
    your full name

_____
    your job title

_____
    your company name

## 08 Mr. Q's Email

Read the following and put yourself in Mr. Q's position. Then write an email using the expressions you've learned.

Mr. Q is the sales manager at MQ Elevator Company. He recently finished the installation of twenty state-of-the-art elevators in a new shopping mall. He wants to write a customer appreciation letter to Sandra Ferrell, construction manager at Northlake Property Group, the company that owns the new mall. Northlake Property is a new client for MQ Elevator, and Mr. Q hopes that Ms. Ferrell will consider his company for future projects.

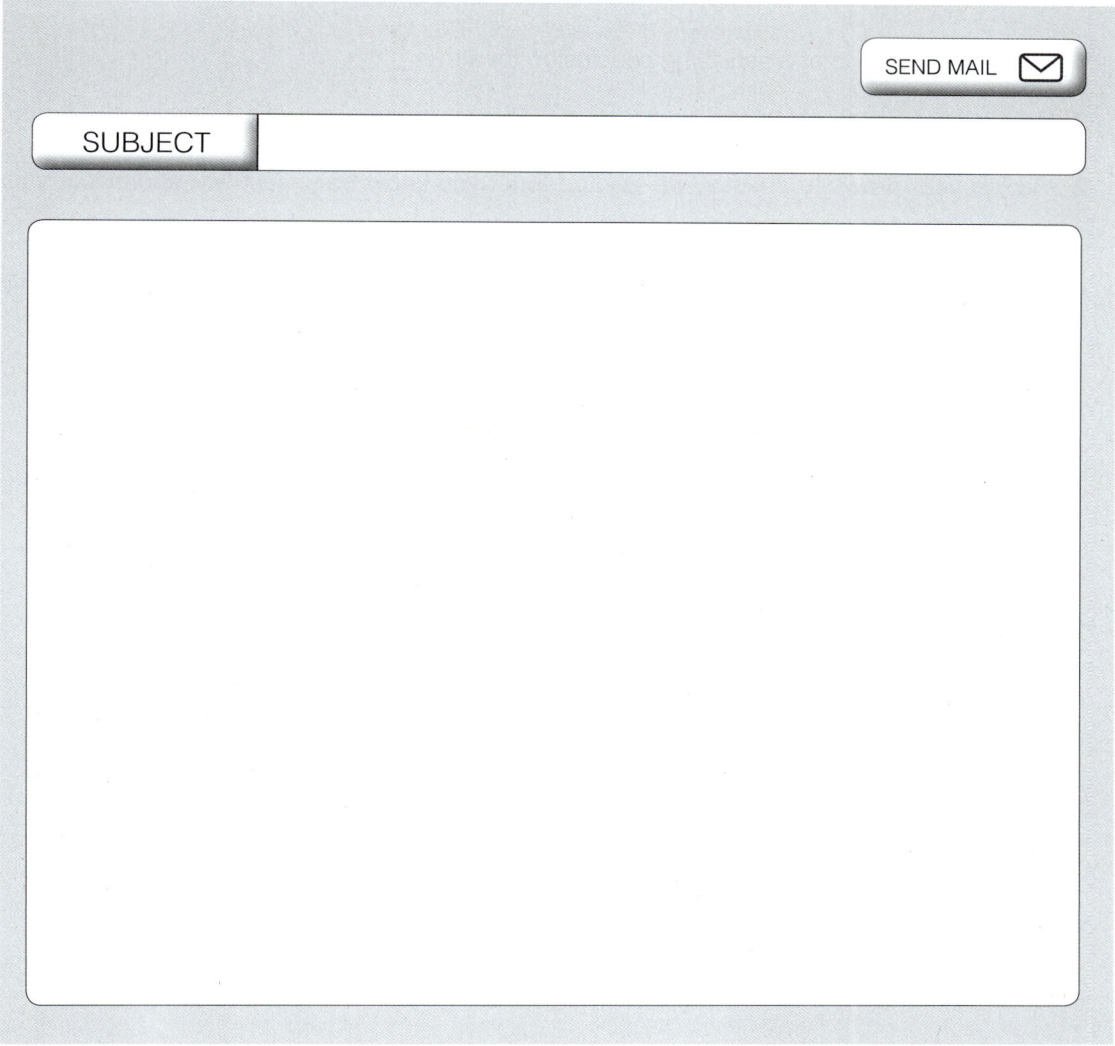

## 09 Exercise

**A  Underline the best word to complete each sentence.**

1  We (share / divide) in your satisfaction of watching the early success in your business.

2  We (recover / recognize) that our success is made possible by partners such as you.


**B  Fill in the blanks with the given words.**

- loyal
- patronage
- long-lasting
- thriving
- profitable
- concerned

1  They finally arrived at a satisfying conclusion for all _____.

2  We look forward to a _____ relationship with your company.

3  As the year draws to a close, we wanted to let you know how much we appreciate your continued _____.

4  We share in your satisfaction of watching your company grow from a new venture into a _____ organization.


**C  Put the words in the right order.**

1  to work | to continue | we | the opportunity | welcome | with you

_____.

2  business partner | several years | a loyal | you | the past | have been | and dependable | over

_____.

3  you | your | our products | are pleased | have made | we | that | premier choice

_____.

4  in the future | very appreciative | and wish you | I | of your assistance | am | continued success

_____.

# Answer Key

# Answer Key

## Unit 01 Promotional Emails

**03 Vocabulary**
A 1. state-of-the-art  2. unveil  3. customizable
  4. in-house

**05 Mini Quiz**
1. We are pleased to inform you about
2. Our company was founded
3. Our company strives to provide
4. We are especially focused on

**06 Email Writing (1)**
1. in-house  2. operating  3. strives  4. requirements
5. state-of-the-art  6. rapidly deployed

**09 Exercise**
A 1. cost-efficient  2. unveil
B 1. in-house  2. operating  3. suit  4. strives to
C 1. We engineer our radiators according to your requirements
  2. This is to inform you that we manufacture industrial rubber hoses.
  3. I'm writing to let you know that we have recently opened a new online store.
  4. You can tour our state-of-the-art facility and try out one of our fitness classes.

## Unit 02 Requesting Samples

**03 Vocabulary**
A 1. request  2. supplier  3. offering  4. availability

**05 Mini Quiz**
1. I am contacting you to request
2. We are hoping to find a new supplier
3. Do not hesitate to contact me
4. Could you provide us

**06 Email Writing (1)**
1. request  2. manufacturing  3. suppliers
4. offerings  5. brochure  6. reach

**09 Exercise**
A 1. inquire  2. hesitate
B 1. provide  2. receive  3. well-known  4. anticipate
C 1. We have recently contacted your company to draw up a contract.
  2. We are also keen to get a promotional brochure.
  3. I am contacting you to request a sample of your product.
  4. We are hoping to find a new supplier as a distributor of our line of cosmetics.

## Unit 03 Sending Samples

**03 Vocabulary**
A 1. recommend  2. release  3. contains  4. inquiry

**05 Mini Quiz**
1. Orders are shipped
2. the lead time is
3. meet your requirements.
4. The following is a guide to

**06 Email Writing (1)**
1. receipt  2. in stock  3. offer  4. containing
5. meet  6. inquiry

**09 Exercise**
A 1. interested  2. regret
B 1. in response to  2. meet  3. acceptable
  4. in connection with
C 1. We appreciate the opportunity to send some of our samples for your review.
  2. Here is our shipping schedule from our factory to your company.
  3. Regarding your request, I propose to send you some sample products.
  4. The lead time is about two weeks from receipt of payment.

## Unit 04 Sending Samples

**03 Vocabulary**
A 1. goods  2. invoice  3. application  4. indicates

**05 Mini Quiz**
1. We'd be glad to receive
2. I would appreciate a quote
3. the following information regarding
4. for quantity purchases

**06 Email Writing (1)**
1. regarding  2. appropriate  3. price quote
4. prompt  5. result in  6. assistance

**09 Exercise**
A 1. discount  2. indicate
B 1. prompt  2. quote  3. standard price  4. receipt

C **1.** Could you provide a firm quote for these goods?
**2.** We'd be glad to receive any relevant information on taxes, shipping, etc.
**3.** We would appreciate a quote on the items listed below.
**4.** Could you give us a reduced rate if we place a bulk order of 100 pieces?

## Unit 05 Sending a Price Quote

### 03 Vocabulary
A **1.** favorable  **2.** confirm  **3.** discount
**4.** terms and conditions

### 05 Mini Quiz
1. Please refer to
2. a more favorable offer.
3. request for a price quote
4. see to your full satisfaction

### 06 Email Writing (1)
1. securing  2. exception  3. quantity
4. favorable  5. place  6. strive

### 09 Exercise
A **1.** discount  **2.** satisfaction
B **1.** confirm  **2.** valid  **3.** refer to  **4.** in response to
C **1.** This is to follow up on your request for a price quote for our product.
**2.** If you need further information, please contact us at 080-1234-5678.
**3.** We are confident that you will not be able to find a more favorable offer.
**4.** If you would like to speak with one of our representatives, please do not hesitate to contact us.

## Unit 06 Filing a Complaint

### 03 Vocabulary
A **1.** inconvenience  **2.** considerable  **3.** shortfall
**4.** consignment

### 05 Mini Quiz
1. in a difficult position
2. make up the shortfall.
3. Much to our dismay
4. file a formal complaint

### 06 Email Writing (1)
1. correctly  2. fulfill  3. considerable
4. perception  5. make up  6. ensure

### 09 Exercise
A **1.** anticipated  **2.** Considerable
B **1.** missing  **2.** complaint  **3.** assurance  **4.** attention
C **1.** This error put our company in a difficult position.
**2.** I'd like to let you know that the goods we ordered have not been supplied correctly.
**3.** I look forward to your prompt response in regards to this matter.
**4.** I would appreciate it if you could make up the shortfall immediately.

## Unit 07 Sending an Apology

### 03 Vocabulary
A **1.** apology  **2.** specifically  **3.** unintentional
**4.** restoration

### 05 Mini Quiz
1. with deep regret
2. taking all the steps we can
3. on behalf of
4. offer sincere apologies for

### 06 Email Writing (1)
1. specifically  2. difficulties  3. steps  4. association
5. discount  6. association

### 09 Exercise
A **1.** request  **2.** unfortunate
B **1.** valued  **2.** ensure  **3.** regret  **4.** apologize
C **1.** I would like to make an apology on behalf of my staff.
**2.** We have been having difficulties with our delivery schedules lately.
**3.** We'll do our best to make it up to you.
**4.** I assure you that we are taking all the steps we can to solve the problem.

## Unit 08 Rejecting a Proposal

### 03 Vocabulary
A **1.** proposal  **2.** stringent  **3.** transactions
**4.** collaborate

# Answer Key

### 05 Mini Quiz
1. hope that we will be able to work together
2. carefully considered your proposal
3. regret to inform you that
4. grateful for your time and interest

### 06 Email Writing (1)
1. appreciate   2. constraint   3. reviewed
4. move ahead   5. accept   6. investing

### 09 Exercise
A  1. grateful   2. impressed
B  1. collaborate   2. vendors   3. analyzed   4. benefits
C  1. Our vendor management team has reviewed your proposal to ensure that it meets our requirements.
2. We regret to inform you that we will be unable to move ahead.
3. We hope that we will be able to work together in the future.
4. I greatly appreciate your interest in our products and welcome the opportunity to do business with you.

## Unit 09 General Notice

### 03 Vocabulary
A  1. disruption   2. patronage   3. closure   4. pertinent

### 05 Mini Quiz
1. Should you have any concerns
2. no later than
3. until further notice
4. is a reminder that

### 06 Email Writing (1)
1. temporarily   2. following   3. timely
4. Should   5. prior to   6. serving

### 09 Exercise
A  1. recommend   2. further
B  1. reminder   2. appreciate   3. beforehand   4. urge
C  1. We would like to thank you for your loyalty and patronage.
2. Counting you among our clients is something for which we are especially grateful.
3. We will do everything in our power to make sure that your orders go out on a timely basis.
4. Should you have any concerns, feel free to email or call us prior to the holiday for customer assistance.

## Unit 10 Notifying Suspension of Service

### 03 Vocabulary
A  1. suspend   2. supplements   3. expedite
4. implication

### 05 Mini Quiz
1. will keep you informed of
2. are committed to doing all we can to
3. will allow us the time to
4. is important to note that

### 06 Email Writing (1)
1. temporarily   2. affect   3. suspension
4. ongoing   5. disruptions   6. committed

### 09 Exercise
A  1. immediate   2. informed
B  1. commitment   2. disruptions   3. recommence
4. adjustment
C  1. We regret to inform you that our service won't be available for the time being.
2. We are committed to doing all we can to resume shipments as soon as we can.
3. The overhaul will surely facilitate our services to you in the future.
4. The suspension of production at the plant will allow us the time to upgrade equipment.

## Unit 11 Submitting a Report

### 03 Vocabulary
A  1. sluggish   2. stabilize   3. enquiries   4. board

### 05 Mini Quiz
1. Once I have your approval
2. is attached herewith
3. The objective of this report is to
4. Attached is a copy of the report on

### 06 Email Writing (1)
1. Attached   2. awareness   3. divided
4. content   5. upcoming   6. hesitate

### 09 Exercise
A  1. objective   2. sources
B  1. deals with   2. Attached   3. enquiries
4. feedback
C  1. The report is divided into three parts

2. Please find attached report you requested yesterday regarding our sales figures.
3. If you have any questions regarding the report, don't hesitate to contact me.
4. A copy of the report on last quarter's sales is attached herewith.

## Unit 12 Scheduling a Meeting

### 03 Vocabulary
A 1. unforeseen  2. resolve  3. budget  4. revisions

### 05 Mini Quiz
1. The meeting will focus on
2. to follow up the discussion
3. to discuss this further
4. to confirm the date and time

### 06 Email Writing (1)
1. planned  2. unforeseen  3. changed
4. detail  5. resolving  6. convenience

### 09 Exercise
A 1. follow  2. discuss
B 1. drop by  2. resolving  3. focus on
4. cover
C 1. I'll contact you again next week to schedule an appointment.
2. This is to discuss the ongoing project and what changes we can make to current plans.
3. Please let me know when you are available this week.
4. I will call your office to inquire about a convenient time and place for the meeting.

## Unit 13 Cancelling a Meeting

### 03 Vocabulary
A 1. setbacks  2. circumstances  3. unavoidable
4. postpone

### 05 Mini Quiz
1. for your patience and understanding
2. Due to unexpected circumstances
3. has forced us to
4. has been moved to

### 06 Email Writing (1)
1. unexpected  2. originally  3. setback  4. less
5. until  6. following

### 09 Exercise
A 1. apologize  2. forced
B 1. available  2. prevent  3. patience
4. set aside
C 1. The meeting has been put on hold until further notice.
2. Please advise us of your availability for attendance.
3. Once again, we would like to apologize for the delay and we hope to see you on May 2.
4. Due to unexpected circumstances, the meeting originally scheduled for March 6 was cancelled.

## Unit 14 Meeting Minutes

### 03 Vocabulary
A 1. presided  2. convened  3. modification
4. minutes

### 05 Mini Quiz
1. were in agreement
2. called the meeting to order
3. made a motion to
4. was presided over by

### 06 Email Writing (1)
1. Attendees  2. order  3. modification  4. standing
5. hold  6. seconded

### 09 Exercise
A 1. order  2. fixed
B 1. presided  2. approved  3. agreement
4. motion
C 1. Meeting convened at 9:30 a.m., Chairman Alfredo Gomez presiding.
2. Meeting adjourned at 1:30 p.m. by chair Jose Domingo.
3. The treasurer presented the latest report on the FCBC's financial standing.
4. Meeting called to order at 12:00 p.m. by chair Deby Davis.

# Answer Key

## Unit 15 Follow-up Email

### 03 Vocabulary
A 1. rectify   2. confident   3. downturn   4. attested

### 05 Mini Quiz
1. are fully aware of
2. I understand your concerns about
3. are a good fit for you
4. I'm positive that

### 06 Email Writing (1)
1. opportunity   2. concerns   3. rectify   4. reduction
5. downturn   6. ventures

### 09 Exercise
A 1. enthusiastic   2. attributable
B 1. positive   2. regardless   3. short   4. attested
C 1. A similar project recently went drastically over budget.
2. I understand your concerns about the recent drops in stock prices.
3. I'm confident that our services are a good fit for you.
4. We appreciate your enthusiastic response and feedback to our offers.

## Unit 16 Executive Summary

### 03 Vocabulary
A 1. upmarket   2. inclination   3. garner   4. generate

### 05 Mini Quiz
1. Our long-term aim is to
2. The purpose of the plan is to
3. Our target clients include
4. We expect to double our sales

### 06 Email Writing (1)
1. upmarket   2. purpose   3. target   4. advantage
5. expand   6. figures

### 09 Exercise
A 1. include   2. generate
B 1. triple   2. aim   3. edge   4. projection
C 1. We're targeting small and medium business owners.
2. This business plan will highlight our progress up until the day of the spa's launch.
3. The purpose of the plan is to secure funding and the finances necessary for the launching of Glo-Spa.
4. We are confident that we will generate up to $25,000 by the end of the first quarter.

## Unit 17 Notifying Contract Termination

### 03 Vocabulary
A 1. clauses   2. violated   3. terminate   4. verbal

### 05 Mini Quiz
1. reserves the right to terminate
2. leaves us no choice but to
3. found to be in violation of
4. bring about a final resolution to

### 06 Email Writing (1)
1. measure   2. continuing   3. satisfactory   4. option
5. communicate   6. unfortunate

### 09 Exercise
A 1. terminate   2. numerous
B 1. Drastic   2. violation   3. verbal   4. inclined
C 1. Our patience has worn too thin to keep this contract.
2. Please contact him to bring about a final resolution to this matter.
3. We reserve the right to terminate the contract without prior notice.
4. Mr. Kim will explain in detail the required paperwork for you to receive your final payment.

## Unit 18 Memorandum of Understanding

### 03 Vocabulary
A 1. assessment   2. conditions precedent
3. due diligence   4. commence

### 05 Mini Quiz
1. is set forth
2. be subject to the fulfillment of
3. be hereinafter referred to as
4. in connection with

### 06 Email Writing (1)
1. according   2. connection   3. transaction
4. precedent   5. subject   6. conduct

### 09 Exercise
A 1. conclude   2. anticipated
B 1. due diligence   2. expire   3. terminated
   4. consideration
C 1. As per the MOU, a contract of sale shall be executed between the parties.
   2. The transaction will be subject to the fulfillment of various conditions precedent.
   3. The consideration amount is set forth in the MOU.
   4. Alpaca granted the Foreign Corporation the option to extend the exclusivity period for an additional 30 days, under certain conditions.

## Unit 19 Sales Contract

### 03 Vocabulary
A 1. irrevocable   2. substantive   3. workmanship
   4. Tariff

### 05 Mini Quiz
1. be the responsibility of
2. to inspect the goods upon
3. give Seller 30 days' advance notice regarding
4. under the foregoing warranty is limited to

### 06 Email Writing (1)
1. otherwise   2. receipt   3. responsibility
4. account   5. acceptance   6. hereunder

### 09 Exercise
A 1. inspect   2. specify
B 1. casualties   2. seek   3. liability   4. advance
C 1. Seller will arrange for delivery through a carrier chosen by Seller.
   2. Seller warrants that the goods sold hereunder are free from substantive defects.
   3. Failure of Buyer to give notice of damaged goods will constitute irrevocable acceptance of the goods by Buyer.
   4. Seller gives 14 days of limited warranty unless otherwise specified, from the date of delivery.

## Unit 20 Thank You Email

### 03 Vocabulary
A 1. dependable   2. profitable   3. esteemed
   4. confidence

### 05 Mini Quiz
1. have been a dependable partner
2. is made possible by
3. look forward to a long-lasting relationship
4. welcome the opportunity to

### 06 Email Writing (1)
1. ability   2. patronage   3. premier
4. thriving   5. meeting   6. satisfying

### 09 Exercise
A 1. share   2. recognize
B 1. concerned   2. long-lasting   3. patronage
   4. thriving
C 1. We welcome the opportunity to continue to work with you.
   2. You have been a loyal and dependable business partner over the past several years.
   3. We are pleased that you have made our products your premier choice.
   4. I am very appreciative of your assistance and wish you continued success in the future.

# POCKET CAMPUS

## 원하는 강의만 골라 담자! 들고 다니는 나만의 캠퍼스

### ▶ 학습과정
외국어는 물론, 학습자들이 글로벌 시대에 갖춰야 할 취업, 인문학, IT, 리더십 등 다양한 지식을 쌓는 캠퍼스로 성장 할 것입니다.

### ▶ Pocket Campus의 특징

**· 합리적인 가격**
강좌당 1만원 안팎의 저렴한 비용으로 학습하실 수 있습니다. 또한 원하는 과정을 장바구니에 담아 자신만의 강좌를 들을 수 있습니다.

**· 다양한 커리큘럼**
HiEnglish 전용교재를 학습할 수 있도록 자체 개발한 모바일 강좌이기에 교재와 함께 학습하기에 최적화 되어 있습니다.

**· 부담없는 학습분량**
한 강좌에 15분 정도 분량이기 때문에 수업에 대한 부담이 없습니다. 동영상 강의를 듣는 학습자들의 학습패턴을 분석하여 적당한 학습 분량을 나누어 구성하였습니다.

 HiEnglish 모바일 학습사이트 포켓캠퍼스    www.pocketcampus.co.kr

## 자동 영문 이력서 작성, 영어 인터뷰 연습
# HiSume

**국내최초!** 외국계 취업, 대기업 영어 면접, 해외 취업을 준비하는 분을 위한 자동 영문 이력서, 영어 인터뷰 연습을 돕는 "HiSume(하주메)" 어플 탄생!

▼ 동영상 강의

▼ 자동 이력서 번역

▼ 영어 인터뷰 연습

▼ 다양한 서비스

### 👍 하주메(HiSume) 무료 서비스
- 주요 외국계 기업 영어 인터뷰 기출 문제 음성 수록
- 국문 이력서와 커버레터를 영문으로 자동 번역
- 영어 인터뷰 답변 녹음 및 정답확인
- 영문 이력서, 커버레터, 영어 인터뷰 등 동영상 강의

### 🎖 하주메(HiSume) 유료 서비스
- 원어민 및 전현직 인사담당자의 이력서, 커버레터 첨삭 지도
- 1:1 영어 인터뷰 코칭

**HiSume 는 이런 사람들에게 필요합니다.**
✓ 외국계 기업 취직을 준비중인 분
✓ 대기업 영어 인터뷰를 준비중인 분
✓ 해외 취업이나 유학을 준비중인 분

**하주메 어플 무료로 다운 받는 법!**
구글 플레이스토어 에서 '하주메(HiSume)' 를 검색 하거나, 하단에 QR코드를 찍는다.

하이유니 홈페이지  www.hiuni.co.kr  전화  070-7169-0708
메일문의  unv3@hiuni.co.kr , market1@hienglish.com